ISBN 978-1-332-71152-9
PIBN 10516530

This book is a reproduction of an important historical work. Forgotten Books uses state-of-the-art technology to digitally reconstruct the work, preserving the original format whilst repairing imperfections present in the aged copy. In rare cases, an imperfection in the original, such as a blemish or missing page, may be replicated in our edition. We do, however, repair the vast majority of imperfections successfully; any imperfections that remain are intentionally left to preserve the state of such historical works.

English
Français
Deutsche
Italiano
Español
Português

www.forgottenbooks.com

Mythology Photography **Fiction**
Fishing Christianity **Art** Cooking
Essays Buddhism Freemasonry
Medicine **Biology** Music **Ancient
Egypt** Evolution Carpentry Physics
Dance Geology **Mathematics** Fitness
Shakespeare **Folklore** Yoga Marketing
Confidence Immortality Biographies
Poetry **Psychology** Witchcraft
Electronics Chemistry History **Law**
Accounting **Philosophy** Anthropology
Alchemy Drama Quantum Mechanics
Atheism Sexual Health **Ancient History**
Entrepreneurship Languages Sport
Paleontology Needlework Islam
Metaphysics Investment Archaeology
Parenting Statistics Criminology
Motivational

A. 1912

Makers of
VIRGINIA HISTORY

Continuation of
South-Western
part of
VIRGINIA
On Same Scale

VIRGINIA

SCALE OF MILES

0 5 10   20   30   40   50

Capitals ✷   County Seats ●   Other Places ●
Railroads_____   Canal_____

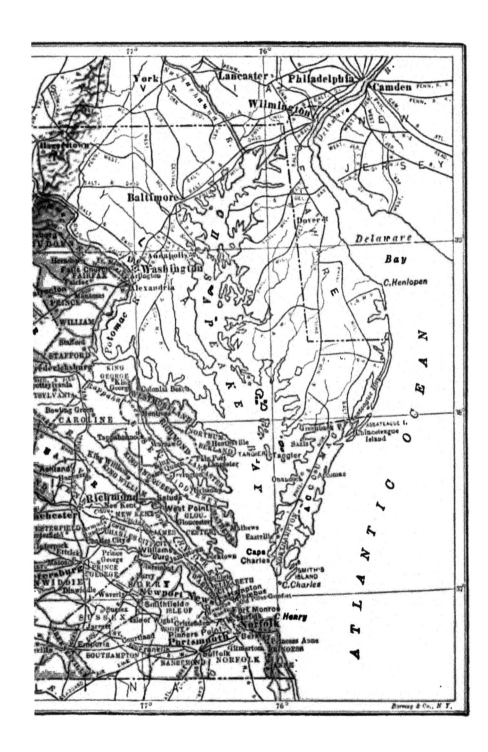

STORIES OF THE STATES

MAKERS

OF

VIRGINIA HISTORY

BY

J. A. C. CHANDLER, LL.D.

EDITOR, VIRGINIA JOURNAL OF EDUCATION

WITH MANY ILLUSTRATIONS AND MAPS

SILVER, BURDETT AND COMPANY

NEW YORK   ATLANTA   BOSTON   DALLAS   CHICAGO

609931

C

PREFACE.

VIRGINIA has been called the "Mother of States and of Statesmen"—a compliment justly due the "Old Dominion." In this little book an effort has been made to give biographical sketches of some of those great leaders who have placed Virginia in the forefront of American states. One great difficulty, however, has presented itself to the author in preparing these sketches: the impossibility of treating the many great men whom our state has produced. When we consider, in addition to those who are treated here, such names as Morgan the Thunderbolt, Wythe, Giles, the Barbours, Cary, Carrington, the many Lees, Doddridge, Baldwin, Tazewell, Taylor, the Masons, Stewart, Leigh, Grayson and scores of others, there seems to be no end to Virginia's distinguished sons. Each locality in the state undoubtedly has some citizen who can truly rank as a maker of Virginia history, though his name is not mentioned in this book. Our purpose, therefore, has been to select only a few characters in the different periods of our history, and to narrate the chief events in their lives in such a way as to give the story of Virginia history from 1607 to the present day. We believe that the best way to teach V.rginia history is by holding up before the boys and girls the deeds of those men who have done so much in the making of our history, and at the same time to give them, on a whole, characters worthy of their imitation. Children should get from their school work laudable ambitions, and there is no better way to stimulate and inspire them than through the history of our great men.

This book may be used in two ways:

(1) *As a history.* It may be put into the hands of the pupils and taught in the same way as any history of Virginia that may be a purely chronological treatment. For this purpose review questions and geography study have been added to each chapter.

(2) *As a supplementary reader.* Every school in Virginia should have a reader which deals entirely with Virginia history, and nothing will be found so profitable and interesting to children as a reading lesson about the men who have made our history.

One result which the author earnestly hopes may be accomplished by this book is a deeper interest in the local history of the state. May every teacher in the state try to find out something about his or her locality, and about the great men of that community. Let this information be taught to the children, and they will grow each day more patriotic. If a spirit of patriotism and of admiration for our great men is firmly imbedded in the youth of our land, then Virginia will have a race of high-minded men in whose hands the future of our dear old Commonwealth will ever be safe.

J. A. C. CHANDLER.

CONTENTS.

ILLUSTRATIONS AND MAPS.

THE WASHINGTON MONUMENT AT RICHMOND, VIRGINIA.

MAKERS OF VIRGINIA HISTORY

CHAPTER I.

JOHN SMITH.

1579–1631.

1. THE ADVENTURER.

VIRGINIA was the first permanent English colony to be planted in America. Its establishment was fraught with difficulty and trials, and it was twenty-seven years from the first undertaking till a colony was founded at Jamestown. The success of the Jamestown settlement was due to Captain John Smith, who, on account of his roving disposition, was called an adventurer.

John Smith was born in 1579 in Lincolnshire, England. His parents, who were of a good English family and of some means, died when Smith was about thirteen years of age. Just before the death of his father, Smith was so anxious for adventure, that he sold his "satchel, books and all that he had, intending secretly to go to sea." His guardian, fearing his foolhardy spirit, bound him as an apprentice to a merchant. He soon left his master and wandered into France, Holland and Belgium, then into Scotland; but finally he returned to his native Lincolnshire, where he lived the life of a hermit and spent his time in riding and shooting.

At length, persuaded by a friend to give up his lonely life, he again crossed to the continent and visited Holland, France, Spain, Italy and Germany, in search of adventure. On his way to France he fell into the hands of some robbers, who took from him all his money and clothes. A few days afterwards, Smith killed one of these robbers in a hand-to-hand encounter.

CAPTAIN JOHN SMITH.

After wandering through France, he set out for Italy. Hardly had the ship put to sea before a terrible storm came up. On board the ship were some pilgrims on their way to visit the holy shrines at Rome. These superstitious persons believed that Smith was a heretical English pirate and that they would perish at sea if he remained with them, so they threw him overboard; but Smith was a good swimmer and reached a little island which was not far away. After many adventures in Italy, Smith determined to go to fight the Turks

More than a hundred years before, the Turks had crossed from Asia into Europe, had conquered Constantinople, and at this time were pushing west into Germany and Austria; the Germans, meanwhile, were fighting to keep them from Vienna. Smith, therefore, proceeded to Germany and joined Prince Sigismund in the struggle against the Turks. He proved a good soldier, and for the aid he rendered to the Germans, he was soon made a captain in the army.

During the war the Germans besieged a town called Regal. To furnish amusement to both armies, a Turkish champion challenged any officer among the Christian forces to fight a single combat with him "for his head." So many of the Christian captains were ready to accept, that a lot had to be cast to decide who should represent the Germans. The choice fell upon Smith. When he went out to meet his opponent, the ladies of the garrison gathered upon the ramparts to see the contest. The Turkish challenger entered the list well mounted and armed, and "on his shoulders were fixed a pair of wings compacted of eagles' feathers in a ridge of silver richly garnished with gold and precious stones." When the sound was given for the charge, Smith rode forth furiously. His lance was so well directed that he pierced the Turk through the beaver which protected his head, the spear point entering his

His Combat with GRVALGO Capt. of Three Hundred Horsemen.

From an old print.

brain.   The Turk fell to the ground, mortally wounded,
whereupon Smith alighted, cut off the head of his antagonist and returned to his troops unhurt.   At once
another Turkish soldier challenged Smith to combat,
and again Smith was victorious.   Then Smith sent a
challenge to the Turks, saying that for further "amusement of the ladies" he would combat with any Turkish
warrior.   This challenge was accepted by a gigantic
Turk, named Grualgo, with the understanding that the
weapons to be used should be pistols and battle axes.
As the contestants rode to the fray, they fired their
pistols and rushed upon each other with their battle
axes.   At a terrible blow from the Turk, Smith lost his

battle axe and came near falling from his horse. The
Turk gave a cry of joy thinking that he had won; but
Smith quickly drew his sword, pierced the Turk through
his back and body, and cut off his head. Thus in three
single combats, Smith overcame three noted Turkish
champions, and proved the truth of his motto, " to
conquer is to live." Prince Sigismund, delighted with
Smith's prowess, promised him a yearly reward of three
hundred ducats ($700), and allowed him to emblazon
upon his coat-of-arms three Turks' heads.

Soon after this
Smith was taken pris-
oner by the Turks,
and sold as a slave.
He fell into the hands
of a Turkish lady of
rank, who became
greatly attached to
her slave. Fearing
that harm might be-
fall Smith from one
of her suitors, she sent
him to her brother

JOHN SMITH'S COAT OF ARMS.

who lived in Tartary, with the request that Smith should
be kindly cared for. But this Turkish nobleman treated
Smith cruelly. Smith's hair and beard were shaven off

and an iron collar was riveted about his neck.   One day he was sent to thresh wheat for his master.   The Turkish nobleman, according to his wont, visited the barn and for no cause gave Smith a severe beating.   Smith was so enraged that he beat out the Turk's brains with the threshing stick.   Dressing himself in the clothes of the Turk, he mounted his master's horse and rode for the Russian frontier, which he reached in sixteen days.   Here he was kindly received and in a short while he started back to his native land.   On his way he stopped to see his friend, Prince Sigismund, who gave him fifteen hundred ducats ($3,500) of gold to replace his loss in the services of Germany.

After traveling in northern Africa and meeting with other adventures, he returned to England in 1604.   At this time all England was filled with talk of Virginia, and many Englishmen were anxious to form a settlement in that land.   Smith, ever ready for new undertakings, offered his services to help plant England's flag on the shores of America.

Review Questions.

Why was Smith called an adventurer ?   Tell of Smith's boyhood.   What experience did he have with robbers in France ?   Tell of how he was thrown overboard into the Mediterranean.   Why were the Germans fighting the Turks ?   Tell of Smith's encounter with three Turks.   Tell of his life as a slave in Tartary.   How did he get back to England ?   What did he hear about in England ?

Geography Study.

Map of Europe.—Find England, Scotland, Holland, Belgium, France, Italy, Spain, Germany, Austria and Turkey. Locate Constantinople, London, Rome and Vienna.   *Map of Asia.*—Find Tartary.

CHAPTER II.

JOHN SMITH.

2. "THE FOUNDER OF VIRGINIA."

WHEN Smith was a boy, he had heard of Virginia, that wonderful country across the Atlantic, where the English had tried to make a settlement under the direction of Sir Walter Raleigh. Before learning of Smith's adventures in Virginia, you should likewise know of Raleigh's attempt to colonize America.

SIR WALTER RALEIGH.

In 1584, Sir Walter Raleigh, a distinguished courtier and scholar, received from Queen Elizabeth a charter allowing him to send settlers to Virginia. Before sending over a colony, Captain Philip Amidas and Captain Arthur Barlow were dispatched with two ships to explore the country.

Amidas and Barlow landed on the coast of the Carolinas on the fourth day of July, 1585, and were greatly impressed with the fertility of the soil and its products. Here they found the melon in its full fruitage, beautiful flowers, and vast forests where roamed the deer and bear, and where birds of beautiful plumage sang melodious songs. From the Indians they heard many stories of the great mountains to the west filled with gold and precious jewels. For the first time, they saw and learned the use of turkeys, potatoes and tobacco. They carried back to England some of these products, and

THE VIRGIN QUEEN.

spread abroad the news of the "good land," which the Virgin Queen Elizabeth named in honor of herself, "Virginia." At that time, Virginia was a vast region described as follows: "The bounds thereof on the east side are the ocean; on the south lieth Florida; on the north Nova Francia (New France); as for the west thereof, the limits are unknown." But the English always held that Virginia ran to the South Sea or Pacific Ocean, which then was thought to be only a few hundred miles west of the Atlantic.   Thus Virginia in its beginning was practically all the present United States.

Raleigh determined to send settlers at once to Virginia, and he experienced no trouble in securing them because of the reports of the wonderful country which contained marvelous wealth.   In 1585, Ralph Lane, as governor, with one hundred colonists, landed at Roanoke Island just off the coast of North Carolina, and began the first English colony in the New World.   The settlement suffered greatly from the Indians, who attempted to destroy it.   When the settlers were on the point of perishing from starvation, they were surprised by a visit from the bold sea captain, Francis Drake, who took them back to England.   Raleigh still felt that Virginia should be settled, and in 1587 sent over a second colony under John White as governor.   White went directly to Roanoke Island where the colonists at once began to rebuild the houses that had been abandoned the year before.   Among the colonists were Mr. Dare and his wife, who was a daughter of Governor White.   Shortly after their arrival a little girl was born to them, and in honor of the country she was named Virginia Dare.   She was the first English child born in America.

Governor White soon returned to England for provisions, but he was detained in England on account of war with Spain. When, after two years' absence, he returned to Roanoke Island, not a man, woman or child could be found. In vain did he search for the colony. On a tree was written the word, " Croatan," which was supposed to mean an Indian village near by, but the neighboring Indians knew nothing of it or of the colonists. In North Carolina to-day, there is a tribe of Indians known as the Croatans, and some think that they have in their veins the blood of Raleigh's colonists,

THE STONE MARKING THE SITE OF OLD FORT RALEIGH.

INSCRIPTION.

On this site in July-August, 1585 (O. S.), colonists, sent out from England by Sir Walter Raleigh, built a fort, called by them "The New Fort in Virginia."

These colonists were the first settlers of the English race in America. They returned to England in July, 1586, with Sir Francis Drake.

Near this place was born, on the 18th of August, 1587, Virginia Dare, the first child of English parents born in America—daughter of Ananias Dare and Eleanor White, his wife, members of another band of colonists, sent out by Sir Walter Raleigh in 1587.

On Sunday, August 20, 1587, Virginia Dare was baptised. Manteo, the friendly chief of the Hatteras Indians, had been baptised on the Sunday preceding. These baptisms are the first known celebrations of a Christian sacrament in the territory of the thirteen original United States.

because many of the Indians of this tribe have light

hair and blue eyes. But this is merely a guess. No one has ever discovered what became of the settlers,

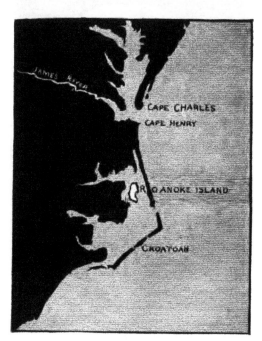

ROANOKE ISLAND, THE HOME OF
THE "LOST COLONY."

and to this day Raleigh's colony is spoken of as the " lost colony of Roanoke."

Raleigh made no further attempts to colonize Virginia, but he always believed that England would occupy the vast region between the St. Lawrence River and Florida and that some day in this fertile territory would be a great English nation. History has shown that Raleigh was a far-seeing man.

For twenty years the colonization of Virginia was laid aside by the English. During this time Queen Elizabeth died, and was succeeded by King James I. The king was learned in books, but without common sense or good judgment; however, when many merchants of his kingdom pressed him with regard to Virginia, he saw that if a successful settlement were made there, it would greatly increase the power of England, and, may be, would add to his own wealth. Moreover, James was a man of true religious impulses and he was anxious that the savages should be converted to Christianity. He consented to form two companies; one called the London Company, and the other the Plymouth Company. To these companies he granted in 1606 a charter, by which the London Company was to be allowed to settle in southern Virginia, somewhere between the Cape Fear (N. C.) and Hudson (N. Y.) rivers. The Plymouth Company was to be allowed to settle in northern Virginia be-

KING JAMES I.

tween what is now the northern boundary of Maine and the mouth of the Potomac River. Both of these companies were trading enterprises, and hoped to find in the New World gold and silver in great quantities, and to acquire much wealth by trading with the Indians.

The London Company determined to plant a colony at once. The chief leaders in the enterprise were Bartholomew Gosnold, a sea captain of great courage and bravery; Sir Thomas Gates and Sir George Somers, two English gentlemen of piety; Robert Hunt, an English clergyman; Edward Maria Wingfield, a prominent London merchant, and Captain Smith. The latter has been called the "soul of the enterprise and the founder of Virginia."

In December, 1606, three small vessels, *Susan Constant, Discovery* and *Godspeed*, sailed down the Thames on their way to Virginia. There were on board, besides the ship's crew, one hundred and five settlers, of whom fifty-four were classed as gentlemen, being men unused to hard work. Only twelve were classed as laborers, the others being goldsmiths, carpenters, perfumers, barbers, masons, tailors, etc. Among the gentlemen were Edward Maria Wingfield, Captain Bartholomew Gosnold, Mr. George Percy, brother of the Earl of Northumberland, Robert Hunt, the clergyman, and Captain John Smith. Hardly had they put to sea before Wingfield charged that Smith intended to "usurp the government, murder the council and make himself king," and caused Smith to be arrested and carried a prisoner to Virginia.

On the 26th of April, 1607, the ships came into the

mouth of the Chesapeake Bay. The capes through which they passed were called Cape Henry and Cape Charles, in honor of the Princes Henry and Charles, the sons of James I. Into the bay flowed a broad river, which was named James, in honor of the king. The

From the painting by Chapman.

THE LANDING OF SETTLERS AT JAMESTOWN.

settlers went up the river and on the thirteenth day of May, 1607, landed on a peninsula, which is now an island, on the north side of the river, and there began the settlement of Jamestown. This was the real beginning of the English colonies in America.

When the settlers started on their voyage to Virginia,

King James did not indicate who should compose the
council to govern the colony, but gave written instructions which were placed in a sealed box, not to be
opened until Virginia was reached.   After entering the
Chesapeake Bay, the colonists opened the box, and
it was found out that Christopher Newport, Bartholomew Gosnold, Edward Maria Wingfield, John Smith,
John Ratcliffe, John Martin and George Kendal were
the members of the council.   According to the instructions, the council proceeded to elect one of their number
as president, and the choice fell upon Wingfield.

At first Smith was not allowed to become a member
of the council because he was still under arrest.   On his
demand, he was granted a trial, at which he proved that
he was not guilty of the charges made by Wingfield, and
he was, therefore, acquitted.   Kendal, who acted as
prosecutor, was condemned to pay Smith two hundred
pounds ($1,000) damages, which the captain generously
presented to the colony.   Smith and his prosecutors
then partook of the holy communion, and Smith was
permitted to take a seat in the council.

The May weather was pleasant and everything
seemed to indicate a prosperous beginning.   At once
the settlers began to build houses.   While waiting for
the erection of a church, an old sail was stretched between some trees for a place of worship, and here the

Rev. Mr. Hunt preached twice every Sunday and read the services daily. It is an interesting fact that of this settlement, which began with religious services, nothing now stands except an old church tower surrounded by some tombstones which are fast crumbling to dust.

The old church tower now to be seen at Jamestown was the part of a church built soon after the settlement had been made.

Hardly had work begun before summer was at hand, and a terrible fever broke out among the colonists. In telling of the suffering of the settlers, George Percy wrote: "Burn-

RUINS OF THE OLD CHURCH TOWER
AT JAMESTOWN.

ing fevers destroyed them. Some departed suddenly, but for the most part, they died of famine. There were never Englishmen left in a foreign land in such misery as we were in this new discovered Virginia. It was indeed a pitiful thing to hear the groaning of the starving and dying." In a few months, more than half of the settlers were dead and among them was Bartholomew Gosnold. Wingfield and Kendal, anxious to escape the ravages of the fever, tried to seize the little boat which belonged to the colonists and to sail back to England. Their design was discovered, and they were at once deposed from the council. Ratcliffe was then elected president of the council in place of Wingfield, but the colonists were as distrustful of him as they had been of Wingfield.

The colony was now greatly in need of food, and so many were ill with fever that it seemed that all would perish. Smith now came to the rescue. He acted with promptness and energy. Going at once to a village near what is now Hampton, he demanded corn of the Indians. When they refused his request, he fired upon them, and captured their god, Okee, which they carried to battle with them. The loss of their god caused the Indians to yield at once to Smith's demand, and they gave him all the corn that he needed. With this he returned to Jamestown in time to save the colony from starvation, and also to prevent Wingfield and Kendal in their second attempt to seize the pinnace.

The colony being well provisioned with the supplies secured from the Indians, Smith now moved up the James River and entered the Chickahominy, looking for a route to the Pacific Ocean, which, according to the

belief of those times, lay but a short way from the
Atlantic. About the last of May, Smith and some others
had gone up the James River as far as the falls where
Richmond now stands. Knowing that he could make
no further progress in his boat up the James, he determined to explore the Chickahominy. In the swamps
of this stream, he lost his companions and was captured
by the Indians, who took him to Opechancanough, the
chief of the Pamunkey tribe.

Smith had with him a circular compass of ivory with
a dial face under glass on either side. He presented
this to the chief, who stood in amazement at the movement of the needle and at the glass which permitted
him to see the needle without touching it. At once
Smith saw his opportunity for making the Indians
stand in awe of him, and by this means he hoped to save
his life. He therefore talked to Opechancanough about
the roundness of the earth, the courses of the sun and
moon, and the use of the compass. The Indians, however, fastened Smith to a tree and were about to shoot
him to death with arrows, when suddenly the old chief
held up the compass, whereupon all the warriors laid
down their arms and untied Smith. At last he was
taken by order of Opechancanough to the latter's
brother, who ruled over the Powhatans, a tribe of Indians living along the James and York rivers. Their

ruler was called after the name of the tribe, Powhatan.

The Powhatan who was ruling at the time that the
English settled in America is described as a sour-looking
man, but tall and well built.   His hair was gray and his
beard was so thin that it seemed none at all.   Although
about sixty years old, he was still able to endure much
hardship.   About his person a guard of forty or fifty
of the tallest men of his country was in constant attendance.

To this Powhatan, who was residing at Werowocomoco
(Gloucester county) on York River, Smith was sent by
Opechancanough.   When Smith was ushered into the
presence of the brawny emperor of the woods, he beheld
him seated before a fire in his royal robe of raccoon skins,
and surrounded by two hundred of his braves.   On either
side of the Indian chief sat a young woman of sixteen
or eighteen years, and behind them were many women
with their heads and shoulders painted red, and their
necks bedecked with great chains of white beads.   As
Smith entered, all the people gave a great shout.   The
Queen of the Appomattox was appointed to bring him
water to wash his hands, and another woman brought
him a bunch of feathers for a towel.   Then the Indians
feasted him on turkey, after which Powhatan and his
warriors held a meeting to decide what should be done

to the Englishman. The conclusion was reached that the white man should be put to death.

While the Indians were consulting, an Indian maiden twelve years old stood looking on. She was the favorite daughter of Powhatan and she was called Pocahontas, which means "bright stream between two hills." She was filled with pity for Smith, and was greatly concerned

From an old engraving.

CAPTAIN SMITH RESCUED BY POCAHONTAS.

when the Indians brought out two large stones and laid Smith's head upon them. Just as the Indians were about to beat out his brains, she ran up, threw herself upon Smith, seized his head in her arms and laid her head upon his.   She thereupon begged her father not to kill Smith.   After much entreaty, the old chief consented to spare Smith's life, and ordered him to make bells and beads for his daughter.   Thus, in an unexpected way, God saved the life of Smith and the first colony of Virginia.

After two days, Powhatan asked Smith to return to Jamestown, and send him two guns and a grindstone. With professions of great friendship, Powhatan furnished Smith twelve guides to conduct him back to the settlement.   They spent the night in the woods, where Smith feared that he would be put to death.   The next morning they reached Jamestown, and the colonists received Smith with great joy and treated the savages with kindness.   Smith showed the Indians two cannon and some grindstones, which he told them to take to their chief.   He caused the cannon to be fired into the trees, and down came the boughs and icicles.   The Indians ran away in fear, but Smith finally persuaded them to return and get the presents and the grindstones which he was sending to Powhatan.

Smith reached the colony at a time when his services were greatly needed.   The people, reduced to forty, were on the point of starvation, and Ratcliffe, who was then president, was a poor leader.   Pocahontas with her attendants came every four or five days, bringing

Smith provisions of venison, turkey and corn. "Her kindness," said Smith, "saved many of the lives that for all else had starved with hunger." The people blessed Pocahontas and loved her for her kindness, but the president and the council began to envy Smith because Powhatan sent him so many presents, and because Pocahontas brought him so many things to eat.

Smith was regarded by the Indians as one who could foretell what would happen. His knowledge of the stars and of the use of the compass had made them believe that he was more than human, and consequently he could do almost anything with them. But when Captain Newport, arriving shortly after this, called upon Powhatan, and attempted to trade with him, the crafty old Indian chief said: "Captain Newport, it is not agreeable to my greatness in a trifling manner to trade with trifles. Therefore, lay down all your commodities and what I like, I will take, and give you what I think fitting their value." Newport did as Powhatan desired, and to his surprise the Indian took all of his trinkets and gave him four bushels of corn, instead of twenty hogsheads, which quantity Newport had expected.

On another occasion Powhatan sent Newport twenty turkeys and asked for twenty swords in return, and Newport actually complied with the request. With

3

Smith, Powhatan had more difficulty. For twenty turkeys which he sent Smith, he did not receive a single sword. He thereupon became angry and planned to destroy Jamestown, but Smith by his watchfulness discovered the plot, and by his firm and stern treatment of the Indians prevented them from succeeding. All the while Pocahontas was befriending the English and showing many kindnesses to Smith.

Shortly after this, Smith went upon an expedition to explore the Chesapeake Bay. He entered the Potomac and Rappahannock rivers and sailed along the Eastern Shore. The accurate map which Smith made of his voyage shows that he was a wonderful navigator. When he returned to Jamestown in September, 1608, he again found the colonists in a frightful condition. Many had died, others were sick, and all the provisions in the storehouse had been ruined by rain. Ratcliffe, the president, had been arrested for mutiny. With these conditions existing, the council and people forced Smith to become president of the colony.

Smith put the colonists immediately to work. The palace that Ratcliffe had begun for himself was torn down, the church and fort were repaired, a roof was put on the storehouse to prevent any further damage to the provisions, and the people were drilled so that they might be prepared for an attack from the Indians.

While these things were going on, Newport arrived
from England with supplies.   Among other presents he
brought a crown and a robe for Powhatan.   King James
had given instructions that Powhatan should be crowned
a king after royal fashion.

Captain Smith was sent to Werowocomoco to tell
Powhatan of his presents, and to invite him to Jamestown to be crowned.   The Indian chief was not at home
when Smith and his companions arrived; so he was sent
for, and, in the mean time, Pocahontas and her women
entertained the Englishmen.   Smith and his companions were seated in an open field before a fire when they
heard a great noise and shrieking.   They seized their
arms, thinking that Powhatan had treacherously planned
to surprise them, but presently Pocahontas came and
assured Smith that no harm was meant, and that she
would suffer death herself before any hurt should befall
him.   Then came thirty young women from the woods,
their bodies painted with many colors, but each one in a
different fashion.   Pocahontas, their leader, had a pair
of buck's horns on her head, an otter's skin at her girdle,
and a bow and arrow in her hand.   The Indian maidens
rushed from the woods with great shouts, and forming
a ring around Smith and his companions, they executed
a peculiar dance.

The next day Powhatan arrived.   He received the

message from Newport, after which, drawing **himself up**
like a great monarch, he said: "If your king **has sent me**
presents, I also am a king and this is my land.   Eight
days I will stay to receive them.   Your father **is to**

THE CROWNING OF POWHATAN.

come to me, not I to him."   Thus Powhatan refused to
go to Jamestown to be crowned, and Captain Newport,
therefore, came to Powhatan's home on York River with
the presents from King James.   After much persuasion
old Powhatan put on the scarlet robe, but when he was
ordered to kneel to receive the crown, he positively re-

fused to bend his knee. "At last, by leaning hard on his shoulders, he a little stooped, and Newport put the crown on his head." The English then fired a salute in honor of Powhatan, the King, who started up with great fear until he saw that no harm was meant.

Smith had much trouble with the settlers because they would not work. Newport had been told in England to get a lump of gold, and so the colony was looking for gold all the time and neglecting the crops. Therefore, the settlers were frequently in great want. Smith complained that there were too many gentlemen among the colonists. He had written a letter to the London Company asking that they send over more laborers, but each new band of settlers contained chiefly gentlemen who were unwilling to work in the fields.

During the winter of 1608-1609, the colony needed corn and other provisions which Smith determined to get from the Indians. As he was going down James River, he met with a friendly Indian who said to him: "Captain Smith, you shall find Powhatan to use you kindly, but trust him not, and be sure he has no opportunity to seize your arms, for he has sent for you only to cut your throat." With this warning Smith proceeded to the home of Powhatan at Werowocomoco. The river was frozen, but he landed by breaking through the ice. When he asked Powhatan for corn, the old

king pretended he did not have any to sell, and valued a
basket of corn at more than he did a basket of copper.
Finally, Powhatan told Smith that the English could
get corn if they would come ashore unarmed, but, if
they brought their arms, the Indians would be afraid
and would not furnish the corn. Smith paid no attention to this, but landed his men with their arms. Then
Powhatan supplied the corn with which Smith loaded
his boats.

Powhatan was now very genial and pleasant and entertained the English with great hospitality. In the
night Pocahontas came through the dark woods and
told Captain Smith of Powhatan's plot. A great feast
of many delicacies had been prepared, and while Smith
and his companions were eating, the Indians would try
to seize their weapons and kill them. She implored
Smith and his men to leave. For her kindness, Smith
offered her many presents, but she would receive none,
and ran away with tears in her eyes. In an hour's
time, eight or ten lusty Indians came with great platters
of venison and other eatables. Fearing poisoned food,
Smith made them taste every dish. He and his companions then enjoyed the feast, and though the Indians
assembled in a great crowd, they did not dare attack the
English, who had their guns by their sides. Thus, from
one place to another Smith went among the Indians,

who held him in great fear. On one occasion, he seized old Opechancanough by his hair and led him out in front of all his braves and placed a pistol at his

JOHN SMITH'S PISTOL.

Now in possession of the Virginia Historical Society.

breast. Of course, he got all the provisions that he wanted.

By the middle of 1609, the colony contained about six plantations, or forts, along the James. Jamestown was the largest, and had about fifty or sixty houses. Among the plantations was West's settlement, near the present site of Richmond. In September, 1609, as Smith was returning to Jamestown from West's plantation, a bag of gunpowder exploded and severely wounded him in the hip. Smith was so crazed by the wound, that he jumped into the water and was rescued by his companions with great difficulty. When he returned to Jamestown, he found a vessel on the point of starting for England. He at once put the government in the hands of George Percy, in order that he might go to London for medical treatment. The colony at the time contained some four hundred and ninety

persons, and was more prosperous than it had been at
any time since its establishment.

Smith never again returned to Virginia, though he
lived twenty-two years longer. For five years he remained quietly in England, but in 1614 he made a voyage to the coast of New England, and was thereafter .
known as "Admiral of New England." The last years
of his life were spent in writing his History of Virginia,
which was published in 1624. He never married. He
died in London in 1631 and was buried in St. Sepulchre's
Church. On his tomb is carved his shield with the three
Turks' heads; and beneath is a long inscription in
poetry of which the following is a part:

> "Here lieth one conquered that hath conquered kings,
> Subdued large territories and done things
> Which, to the world, impossible would seem
> But that truth is held in more esteem.
>
> Oh, say may his soul in sweet Elysium sleep
> Until the keeper that all souls doth keep
> Return to judgment, and that after thence
> With angels he shall have his recompense."

Smith was undoubtedly a true and noble man, and
the colony of Virginia would have prospered from the
first had his advice been taken. But, unfortunately,
the colonists had the fever for gold, and spent their time
in searching for it, finding only some yellow dirt, which

they ignorantly took for the precious metal.   If the time consumed in digging and looking for gold had been devoted to building homes and cultivating the soil, there would never have been so much suffering in the colony. Smith pleaded with the colonists to work.   He told them that they would acquire wealth neither by trading with the Indians nor by finding gold, but by producing such crops as they could ship to England and sell there.   Truly he had the right idea of what would make a permanent and prosperous colony.

Review Questions.

Tell of Raleigh's settlements in Virginia.   Who was Virginia Dare?   Tell of the charter of the Plymouth and London companies.   What men were instrumental in settling Virginia?   What ships started for Virginia in 1606?   What was the character of the settlers?   Who were the leading men? Where and when was the first settlement made?   Tell of Smith's arrest and trial.   Tell of the first church in Virginia. What only remains now at Jamestown?   Tell of the summer of 1607.   How did Smith get food in 1607?   Tell of his trip up the Chickahominy.   Tell of his experience with Opechancanough and the compass.   Describe Powhatan.   Tell of the way Smith was received by Powhatan.   How did Pocahontas save him?   Tell of the Indians' experiences with the cannon and the grindstones.   Tell the difference between the way in which Smith and Newport traded with the Indians.   What waters did Smith explore?   Tell of Smith as president of the colony.   Describe the entertainment which Pocahontas gave to Smith.   Tell of the crowning of Powhatan.   Describe Smith's experiences during the winter of 1608-1609.   Why was Smith forced to return to England?   Tell of his life after leaving Virginia, and of his death.   Write a composition on Smith.

Geography Study.

Map of the United States.—Find North Carolina, Florida and Virginia. Locate Roanoke Island. *Map of Virginia.* Find Cape Henry, Cape Charles, James River, Jamestown, Chickahominy River, Richmond, Pamunkey River, York River, Werowocomoco, Potomac River, Rappahannock River and Chesapeake Bay.

CHAPTER III

POCAHONTAS.

1595(?)–1617.

IN connection with the life of Smith you have learned something of the Indian maiden Pocahontas. Her story is a most interesting one. She was far above her race in thought and feeling. She was not treacherous and cruel, but kind and gentle. Though a savage, she was a high-minded woman and deserved the title of "Lady Rebecca," or the "Lady Pocahontas." You can not understand how great a

THE INDIAN MAIDEN, POCAHONTAS.

woman she was, unless you know something of her people.

The ancient inhabitants of Virginia were called Indians because Columbus had given the natives of America

that name.   Virginia was not populous, and among the
Indians were many more women and children than men.
Within sixty miles of Jamestown were some five thou-
sand natives divided into several tribes, the most impor-

AN INDIAN IN SUMMER
DRESS.

tant being the Monocans, the Pa-
munkeys and the Powhatans.

The Indians were usually tall
and straight and "of a color brown
when they were of age, but they
were born white.   Their hair was
generally black but few had any
beard.   The men wore one-half of
their beard shaven, the other half
long.   For barbers, they used their
women, who with two shells grated
away the hair in any fashion they
pleased."   The women were hardy
and could endure much cold and
hunger.   They worked the corn
and raised the tobacco, while the warriors or braves
would hunt and fish.

The clothes of the Indians were made of the skins of
wild animals; their finest garments were of deer skin,
often embroidered with white beads.   The poorer among
the Indians made clothes of grass and of the leaves of
trees, and sometimes they tied together turkey feathers

for clothing. They painted themselves in many colors, and both men and women wore long chains and bracelets in their ears. A certain charm was supposed to reside in the snake, so that often an Indian brave wore through holes in his ears, a small greenish yellow-colored snake nearly one-half yard in length, which would crawl and lap about his neck and kiss his lips. On their heads the Indians often had the wings of birds or some large feather with a rattle.

AN INDIAN FAMILY AT HOME.

The homes of the Indians were, for the most part, near rivers and not far from some fresh stream of water. Their houses, called wigwams, were built with the boughs of trees like our arbors and covered with mats or bark. Around these wigwams there were often from twenty to two hundred acres of cleared land, for the production of Indian corn and tobacco. The chief food was fish, turkeys, squirrels and green corn; in winter the Indians grated their corn, of which they made hominy. They used the bow and the arrow and had boats called canoes, which were hollowed from large logs by burning. Their religion consisted chiefly in the worship of fire, water, lightning and thunder and a god called Okee, whom they served more from fear than from love.

In war the Indians were treacherous and cruel, and their great delight was to scalp their enemies. They avoided open warfare and would never forgive an injury. They were not trustworthy, being full of deceit; yet from such a race sprang Pocahontas, a woman whose name will always be honored in Virginia.

Pocahontas was true, gentle and noble. When she was a child about twelve years of age she saved Smith's life, and afterwards she time and again furnished the white settlers with provisions. On another occasion, as you will remember, when Smith was trying to get corn from Powhatan, Pocahontas came and informed Smith that the Indians were planning to kill him. To give Smith this warning was a brave deed, for had her action been discovered by the Indians, she would undoubtedly have been put to death.

After Smith's departure from Jamestown, Pocahontas did not again visit the whites and they greatly missed her kindness to them. Old Powhatan seemed to fear that she might fall into the hands of the English; therefore he sent her for safety to a friendly chief, Japazaws, who lived on the Potomac River. In 1612, Captain Argall went into the Potomac country to trade with the Indians for corn, and while there, he learned that Pocahontas was in that region. He thereupon gave a copper kettle to Japazaws to betray her into his hands. After much persuasion Pocahontas consented to go with Japazaws and his wife to the English boat to see how it was constructed. When she had got aboard, Argall informed her that she was his prisoner. Though she begged in tears for her release, Argall would not relent, but took her to Jamestown.

Argall's purpose in making a prisoner of Pocahontas was to force Powhatan to release seven of the English whom he had held as prisoners and to secure greater supplies of corn for the liberation of his daughter. Powhatan released the prisoners, but as he did not send the corn, the English still retained Pocahontas at Jamestown. She was kindly treated, and was taught the Christian religion, and after a short time was baptized under the name Rebecca. While Pocahontas was being instructed in Christianity, Mr. John Rolfe, a widower, fell in love with her and after about a year won her consent to marry him. Many people have thought that she loved John Smith, as she asked about him so frequently, and it seems that the good people of Jamestown deceived the girl by telling her that Smith was dead.

The marriage was performed by the Rev. Mr. Whitaker at the Jamestown church, in April, 1613. At that time marriages were not frequent in Virginia, because, as yet, few women had come to the colony. The first marriage in the colony took place at Jamestown, in December, 1608, when Anne Burras became the wife of John Laydon. That marriage had undoubtedly interested the people, but when Rolfe led Pocahontas to the altar as his bride, the whole colony felt concerned, because it meant the union of an English gentleman and an Indian Princess. From this marriage the settlers hoped for perpetual peace with the Indians.

Powhatan was informed of the proposed marriage, and gave his consent, but he feared the whites, and would not go to Jamestown to witness the ceremony. He sent an uncle and two brothers of Pocahontas. Powhatan and the neighboring Indians made peace with the whites, which peace lasted till the death of Pocahontas, or the Lady Rebecca, as she was often called. It is said that Sir

Thomas Dale, who was then governor of Virginia, was so pleased with this marriage, that he sent a messenger to Powhatan asking for the hand of a younger sister of Pocahontas. Thus Dale wished to make stronger the bonds of peace and friendship between the whites and the Indians. To the messenger Powhatan said, "I gladly accept your salute of love and peace, which, while I live, I shall exactly keep. His (Dale's) pledge thereof I receive with no less love, although they are not so great as I have received before. As for my daughter, I have sold her within these last few days to a great chief, three days journey from me, for two bushels of rawrenoke." To this speech of the savage chief, the messenger replied: "I know your highness by returning the rawrenoke might call her back again to gratify your brother, Sir Thomas Dale, and the rather, because she is but twelve years old. Besides its forming a bond of peace, you shall have in return for her three times the value of the rawrenoke in beads, copper and hatchets." But Powhatan declined this tempting offer, saying: "No, I love my daughter as my life; and, though I have many children, I delight in none so much as her, and if I should not often see her, I could not possibly live; and, if she lived at Jamestown, I could not see her, having resolved on no terms to put myself into your hands or come among you. Therefore, I desire you to urge me no

4

further. . . . From me he (Dale) has a pledge, one
of my daughters, which so long as she lives shall be
sufficient. When she dies, he shall have another. I
hold it not a brotherly part to desire to bereave me of
my two children at once. . . . This, I hope, will
satisfy my brother. Now, since you are weary, and I
sleepy, we will here end."

From a painting by Sully.

LADY POCAHONTAS.

In 1616, Rolfe visited England, taking with him the
Lady Pocahontas. A news letter of the day said, "Sir
Thomas Dale has arrived from Virginia and brought

with him some ten or twelve old and young of that country, among whom is Pocahontas, a kind of cazique of that country, married to one Rolfe, an Englishman." Pocahontas had learned to speak English well and her manner was that of a refined English lady.

In England she met Captain Smith, and the story of their meeting is best told in Smith's own words: "Being about this time preparing to sail for New England, I could not stay to do her that service I desired—but hearing that she was at Brentford—I went to see her. After a modest salutation, without a word she turned about and obscured her face, not seeming well contented—but not long afterwards, she began to talk—saying: 'You did promise Powhatan what was yours should be his, and I liked you. You called him father being in his land a stranger, and for the same reason so must I do you,' which, though I would have excused, I durst not allow that title because she was a king's daughter. With a well set countenance, she said: 'Were you not afraid to come into my father's country and caused fear in him and all his people but me, and fear you here I should call you father? I tell you I will, and you shall call me child, and I will be for ever and ever your country woman. They did tell us always you were dead and I knew no other till I came to Plymouth. Yet Powhatan did command Uttomatomakkin* to seek you and to know the truth, because your countrymen will lie much."

Smith at once wrote a letter to Queen Anne, the wife of James I., asking her to take an interest in the Lady Rebecca and in this letter for the first time he described

QUEEN ANNE, WIFE OF JAMES I.

how she saved his life at the risk of her own. An old historian tells us: "She was carried to Court by the Lady Delaware and entertained by ladies of the first quality towards whom she behaved herself with so much grace and majesty, that she confirmed the bright character Captain Smith had given of her. The whole court was charmed with the decency and grandeur of her deportment, so

*This was one of the Indians, a brother-in-law of Pocahontas, who went to England with her. Powhatan instructed him to number the English. He got some sticks when he landed and began to cut a notch for every Englishman that he saw, but he soon gave up in despair as they were so many.

much so that the poor gentleman, her husband, was threatened to be called to account for marrying a princess Royal without the king's consent." She went to many balls, plays and entertainments held in her honor. What a change from a savage in the wilderness of Virginia!

In March, 1617, John Rolfe prepared to embark for Virginia, but his wife was suddenly taken ill and died

THE SUPPOSED GRAVE OF POWHATAN, FATHER OF POCAHONTAS.

at Gravesend, in the County of Kent. She was buried there in the chancel of the church. The old church was burned in 1727, and there remains no monument to her memory. Pocahontas left one son, Thomas Rolfe, who later returned to Virginia and became a planter. His only child, Jane, married Colonel Robert Bolling,

from whom many of the prominent families of Virginia
are descended.   Among the descendants of Pocahontas
was John Randolph of Roanoke.

Pocahontas, though by birth a savage, readily acquired
the culture and refinement of the English, for she was by
nature a noble woman.   Virginia should always honor
her memory because, through her kindness and Smith's
bravery, the colony was saved from destruction.   The
names of John Smith and Pocahontas are for this reason
inseparably connected.

Review Questions.

Tell of the Indian tribes of Virginia.   **Describe the appear-**
ance and dress of an Indian.   Tell of the **homes and food** of
the Indians.   What sort of people were they in **disposition!**
Tell how Argall captured Pocahontas.   How was **Pocahontas**
treated at Jamestown?   Tell of her baptism and **marriage.**
Tell of Powhatan's reply to Dale when he asked for the
younger daughter of Powhatan.   Tell of the meeting of **Smith**
and Pocahontas in England.   How was Pocahontas received
at court?   Tell of her death.   What do you know of her
descendants?

Geography Study.

Map of England.—Find Plymouth, London, County of
Kent and Gravesend.

CHAPTER IV

EDWIN SANDYS.

1561–1629.

VIRGINIA did not prosper rapidly in its early days because the London Company was badly managed, and did not send the proper tools and supplies to the settlers. Smith, as you remember, complained to the Company, and urged it to adopt a more liberal policy. No decided change, however, was made until Sir Edwin Sandys became treasurer of the Company. But from Smith's departure from Virginia to

Sandys's election was a period of ten years, during which time the colony was, on a whole, governed in a despotic way, and was often on the verge of ruin.

When Smith left Virginia in 1609, the government was placed in the hands of George Percy, who was unable to manage the colonists. The Indians at once began to destroy the outlying settlements, because there was no Smith to keep them in mortal fear. The supplies were either wasted or destroyed, and the settlers often had to live on roots and acorns and the skins of horses. It is even said that some ate the body of an Indian who had been killed in war, having first boiled it with roots and herbs. Another horrible story is told of a man who killed his wife and was discovered eating her body. For this crime he was burned to death. Out of more than four hundred and ninety men whom Smith had left in Virginia, in six months "there remained not past sixty men, women and children, most miserable and poor creatures." Just at this time (1610) Gates and Somers arrived.

About six months before Smith returned to England, Sir Thomas Gates and Sir George Somers had sailed from London to bring fresh supplies and additional settlers to Virginia. They were driven by a terrible storm, and their ship, the *Sea Venture*, was wrecked upon the Bermudas. Here they succeeded in constructing two small boats, *Patience* and *Deliverance*, in which they reached Virginia. Great was the joy of the starving colonists, as the two vessels sailed up the James. When the new arrivals came ashore, the few remaining settlers crowded around them and begged that they might be taken back to England. Since there were no provisions upon which the colony could live, Gates and Somers agreed that Jamestown should be abandoned. Having buried all their arms and ammunition at the gate of the fort, the colonists went aboard the ships and set sail for England.

LORD DELAWARE.

It looked as if the Virginia colony was doomed, but God had willed otherwise. Scarcely had the ships gotten out of sight of Jamestown, before they met a small boat which announced that Lord Delaware had come out from England to assume command of the Virginia colony, and that a new government would be established. At once Gates and Somers returned to Jamestown; and three days later (June 10, 1610), Lord Delaware arrived with three vessels. As he landed upon the shore, he

knelt and offered silent prayer to God. He then summoned the people to the church, where the Rev. Mr.
Bucke preached. By Lord Delaware's opportune arrival the colony of Virginia was again saved from ruin.

Smith, on reaching England in 1609, told the London
Company that the only hope for Virginia was a strong
government. The King granted a new charter to the
Company then composed of 659 persons and 56 trading
guilds or companies. By this charter Sir Thomas
Smythe was named as treasurer. The company at once
decided to send to the colony a governor. The choice fell
upon Thomas West, Lord Delaware, who was the first
man to have the title of governor of Virginia.

Immediately after his arrival, Delaware informed the
people that they would be governed mildly but firmly.
The idle were put to work and the hours of labor were
fixed from six to ten in the morning, and from two to
four in the afternoon. Delaware also caused the church
to be repaired and had two sermons preached every
Sunday and one on Thursday. Every day at ten o'clock
the church bell was rung and the people attended
prayers. Again at four o'clock in the afternoon they
were required to be at services. "On Sunday, when
the governor went to church, he was accompanied by
the councillors, officers, and all the gentlemen with a
guard of halberdiers in his lordship's livery, handsome

red cloaks, to the number of fifty on each side and behind him. In the church his lordship had his seat in the choir in a green velvet chair, with a cloth and also a velvet cushion laid on the table before him on which

A VIEW OF DUTCH GAP.

he knelt. The council and officers sat on each side of him, and when he returned to his house, he was escorted back in the same manner."* Jamestown at this time was only a small village of rude wooden houses, and such ceremony as became a king appeared very foolish in Virginia. Still it helped to increase Lord Delaware's power; and it made the people stand in awe of him and obey his laws.

* See Campbell's "History of Virginia," p. 102.

After a few months, Delaware returned to England, and was succeeded by Sir Thomas Dale who remained governor for about five years. He governed with a hand of iron, and under him the colony prospered greatly. During Dale's rule, several new plantations were formed, among them being Henrico City, built at what is now known as "Dutch Gap," upon a neck of land not far from Richmond, where James River makes a great bend of seven miles and "returns to one hundred and twenty yards from the point of departure."

Dale made a wonderful change in the mode of living which had previously prevailed in the colony. Before his time, since all the land was owned by the London Company and all the settlers were sent out by it, the lands were worked in common and all the products —and these belonged to the company—were put into one store house. Dale changed this by assigning to every man three acres of land, which he could hold as his own provided he paid a yearly rent to the company of two and one-half barrels of corn. This change produced good results, for each settler now had the opportunity to make something for himself, if he would work.

With Dale came the Rev. Alexander Whitaker, a graduate of Cambridge University, England. His great desire was to convert the Indians to Christianity, and through his influence an attempt was made at Henrico

City to build a college, chiefly for the education of the Indians. This was the first American college, and it was destroyed during the Indian massacre of 1622.

When Dale returned to England in 1616, he was succeeded by George Yeardley as deputy-governor, who gave great satisfaction to the Virginians, but after a year the government passed into the hands of Samuel Argall.

Virginia was just beginning to prosper; but under Argall came a change, for he seized all the public warehouses and appropriated the grain and tobacco to his own use. He forced the laborers to work for him, instead of for the Company. In those days there were some persons in Virginia ("indented" servants) who, in order to get their transportation to the colony, had bound themselves for a period of years, some for three, some for five and some for ten years. When they had served the time for which they were bound, they became free citizens of Virginia, but Argall was such a tyrant that he kept in bondage some men who had served out their terms. Such arbitrary rule caused the colony again to decline, and at once the London Company recalled him.

By this time the factions in the London Company were becoming more distinct. Argall was a relative of Sir Thomas Smythe, and many members of the Com-

pany felt that if Smythe was removed, the Company
would manage the affairs more satisfactorily. By the
charter of 1609, the officers and councilors of the Company were appointed by King James, but in 1612, when

a third charter was
granted, the London Com-
pany was given the right
to elect its own officers.
There soon came to exist
in the Company a liberal
party which felt that the
government of Virginia
should be run without
interference from the
king. To the party of
the court belonged Sir
Thomas Smythe, while
the leader of the King's
opponents was Sir Edwin
Sandys, who was finally

SIR THOMAS SMYTHE.*

elected treasurer of the London Company (1619).

Sandys was born in 1561. He was a son of Edwin
Sandys, Archbishop of York, and was educated at Ox-

* This portrait and those on pp. 55 and 64 are taken from Fiske's
"Old Virginia and Her Neighbors," by permission of the publishers,
Messrs. Houghton, Mifflin and Company.

ford University where he received the degree of Bachelor of Arts. When a young man, he became a member of Parliament where he was well known for his oratory and scholarship. Here he allied himself with those who opposed the King's high-handed methods of governing. From 1617 to 1619 Sandys was deputy-treasurer of the London Company.

When Sandys became treasurer in 1619, he determined to give Virginia a better government. For this purpose Yeardley was made governor, and representative government was introduced. The sending of young women to the colony to become wives of the settlers was also one of Sandys's schemes. In order that the tobacco industry of

EARL OF SOUTHAMPTON.

Virginia might be encouraged, he favored the exclusion of all tobacco from England not grown in Virginia.

These measures did not please the despotic King

James, and he, therefore, wished to get Sandys out of the treasurership of the Company.   In 1620, when the election was at hand, the members of the Company were about to reëlect Sandys, when some representatives of the king came to the meeting and commanded, in the king's name, that some other person should be selected.

NICHOLAS FERRAR.

Filled with indignation, the liberals called for the reading of the Charter. When the document had been read, one of the members said: "The words of the charter are plain; the election of a treasurer is left to the free choice of this Company." Sir Edwin Sandys, hoping to preserve peace, withdrew his name, but caused his friend the Earl of Southampton to be elected, though the King had nominated Sir Thomas Smythe.   Southampton was a friend of the great Shakespeare, and a member of the liberal party.   Associated with the earl as deputy-treasurer was Nicholas Ferrar, a graduate of Cambridge and a deeply religious man.

Southampton, Sandys and Ferrar were the ruling spir ts of the London Company and they firmly insisted that the Virginians should be allowed self-government. The king, therefore, determined to destroy the London Company, and after a struggle of four years the charter of the Company was taken away (1624). Southampton, Sandys and Ferrar barely escaped imprisonment on account of their resistance to the King. When Ferrar saw that the Company was doomed, he had a copy made of the proceedings of the Company from the day (April 28 1619) that Sandys was elected treasurer till the overthrow of the Company in 1624. This copy is now preserved in the Library of Congress at Washington.

The Earl of Southampton died a few months after the overthrow of the London Company. Sandys lived till 1629, and during his latter years was a prominent member of Parliament. Nicholas Ferrar lived till 1637. For the last eleven years of his life he was a preacher, and did much in England to promote education and to encourage philanthropy. Southampton, Sandys and Ferrar never came to America, but they deserve our gratitude for having preserved representative government in Virginia.

Review Questions.

What horrible things occurred at Jamestown after Smith left? Tell of the shipwreck of Gates and Somers. What was the condition of the colony when Gates and Somers arrived? Tell how Delaware saved the colony from destruction. Tell of Delaware's government of Virginia. Tell of Dale's rule in

Virginia.   What was the first attempt to establish a college?
Tell of Argall's rule in Virginia.   Give an account of the fac-
tions in the London Company.   Tell of the life of Edwin
Sandys.   What did he do for Virginia?   Tell of the Earl of
Southampton.   Give some account of Nicholas Ferrar.   Tell
of the overthrow of the London Company.   Why should
Southampton, Sandys and Ferrar be remembered?

Geography Study.

Map of United States.—Find the Bermuda Islands.   *Map
of Virginia.*—Locate Dutch Gap, Richmond and Jamestown.

CHAPTER V.

GEORGE YEARDLEY.

1580(?)–1627.

As you have learned, it was chiefly through the influence of Sir Edwin Sandys that representative government was granted to Virginia, but its inauguration in Virginia was acccmp ished by Sir George Yeardley.

Yeardley was born in London about 1580. His father was a merchant tailor. Of his early life, very little is known. He sailed for Virginia in 1609 along with Gates and Somers and with them was shipwrecked on the Bermudas. During Dale's administration, Captain Yeardley became one of the inhabitants at Lower Bermuda Hundred, a settlement on James River, and was soon one of the leading men of the colony.

In 1616 the colony seemed to be somewhat declining. There were now only three hundred and fifty people distributed among seven settlements, whereas five years before, there had been seven hundred people in Virginia. The cause of this decline was the fact that nothing as yet had been produced in Virginia which would yield wealth. The colony had been planted with the hope of finding gold and making money by trading with the Indians. Food supplies were brought from England instead of being raised in Virginia. Smith had insisted that grain should be raised, and in 1608 had caused forty acres to be planted in Indian corn. Farming was difficult because the settlers had no ploughs,

A VIRGINIA TOBACCO FIELD OF TO-DAY.

and the land was cultivated with the spade, shovel and the hoe. When Dale came to Virginia, he forced the settlers to plant corn, and he brought over many hogs, cows and horses. In 1612, the colonists began the cultivation of tobacco, but only in patches of a few plants.

At this time nothing had been shipped from Virginia, except a little sassafras root. A great deal of tobacco was used in England, but it was brought from the West Indies and South America. It is said that the first Virginian who attempted the planting of tobacco with the view of shipping it to England was John Rolfe, the husband of Pocahontas. Yeardley believed that the wealth of Virginia lay in the production of tobacco, and as soon as he got the reins of the government, he exerted himself to increase its cultivation. As a result, a large crop was planted in 1617 and the colonists were so anxious to raise tobacco, that it was grown even in the streets of Jamestown. After a year Yeardley returned to England, yielding the deputy-governorship to Argall, who held the position for two years.

Yeardley was very popular in Virginia and England, and for some reason King James I. had knighted him. When Sandys became treasurer of the Company, Yeardley was appointed Governor and Captain-General of Virginia, and in April, 1619, he returned to Virginia. Under him the colony took on new life. A great number of settlers came, and the four hundred inhabitants of 1618, by the close of 1619, had increased to two thousand.*

---

* In 1619 many emigrants were coming from England, but only a few of them were women. It was seen that Virginia could not

Yeardley brought with him instructions from the
London Company to establish a better form of government for the people of Virginia and "that the planters
might have a hand in the governing of themselves, it
was granted that a general assembly should be held
yearly once, whereat were to be present the Governor
and council, with two burgesses from each plantation
freely to be elected by the inhabitants thereof." This
assembly was empowered to make such laws as should
seem best for the government of the colony. Carrying
out his instructions, Yeardley issued a call to the people
of Virginia to elect representatives to meet at Jamestown on Friday, the thirtieth day of July, 1619. At
the time named, the general assembly, better known
as the House of Burgesses, met for the first time in the
history of Virginia. This was also the first legislative

prosper unless many home builders came to the colony; therefore,
the London Company sent to Virginia ninety girls who were to become wives of the settlers. The expense of sending them was large
and as they were without means to pay their own transportation, it
was understood that when these girls arrived in Virginia, any man
who paid one hundred and twenty pounds of tobacco, about eighty
dollars, should be entitled to select one of the girls as his wife
When the shipload of young women arrived at Jamestown, the
planters from the settlements flocked there seeking wives to take to
their homes. The outcome of this experiment was that other women
soon came to the colony, and in a little while the majority of the men
were married and had made Virginia their permanent homes. Up to
this time the colonists were chiefly single men who had come to Virginia with the desire of making a fortune in order that they might
return to live in England.

body to be held on American soil. In this assembly
were twenty-two representatives, two being elected from
each of the eleven settlements then in the colony.

It was indeed a happy day when the House of Burgesses came together to pass laws for the colony
which was in the course of years to bloom into a great
republic. Since there was no capitol building at Jamestown, the governor and council had to decide upon a
place of meeting. The church was selected as the most
convenient place. To this the governor and council and
burgesses went in the order of their official positions.
The governor entered first and sat down in his accustomed place, then next to him, on either side, came all
the members of the council, except the secretary of the
council, who was appointed speaker; he sat directly
in front of the governor. A secretary was appointed
who sat next to the speaker, and in front of the bar stood
the sergeant-at-arms ready to execute any command of
the assembly. Before any business was transacted, the
governor asked Mr. Bucke, the minister, to offer prayer
for God's blessing on the deliberations of the assembly.
Then all the burgesses, before they were admitted to a
seat in the choir of the church, were requested to retire
to the body of the church, and each man was called in
order and by name, and was brought before the speaker's
desk and required to take the oath acknowledging the

King of England as the head of the Church as well as
of the State. After having made the oath, each burgess
was seated as a member. Thus began the first Virginia
legislature. It remained in session five days. The
governor sat with it throughout the whole session, a
right which the governor does not have in these modern
days.

The House of Burgesses petitioned the London Company that every man might own the land which he cultivated, and that proper steps should be taken toward
the erection of a college in the colony. A law was
passed making tobacco the money of the colony, and for
a long time after this the people used tobacco in buying
and selling goods. The burgesses and the preachers received their pay in tobacco; and with it ladies bought
their silks and embroidery. The first House of Burgesses
enacted that any man found idle should be forced to
work, and that the authorities should appoint a master
for him. Every gambler should be fined. Any man
who was found drunk, for the first offense, was to be reproved in private by the minister; for the second offense,
he was to be reproved in public in the church, and for
the third time, he was to be imprisoned for twelve hours.
If this did not cure him of drunkenness, he should be
severely punished as the governor and the council should
see fit. It was also provided by law that no man should

wear expensive clothing. For extravagance in living, a person was forced to contribute to the church according to his dress.

It is worthy of note that the same year which saw the establishment of the first House of Burgesses and the beginning of so many permanent homes, should likewise have seen the introduction of negro slavery. In August, 1619, Jamestown was visited by a Dutch man-of-war which sold to the settlers twenty negroes. Of these, Governor Yeardley himself bought eight, five women and three men. The planters who owned these slaves did not think that they were committing a sin, for at that time slavery existed in some form or other in all parts of the world. In

STOVE USED IN THE HOUSE OF BURGESSES IN THE EARLY EIGHTEENTH CENTURY.

Virginia there were a number of white men who were practically slaves. They were called "indented servants," because they had been bound by an indenture for a fixed number of years. Some .

of these servants had been bound in this way because they had committed crimes, while others had of their own accord agreed to be servants in order that they might come to Virginia. While they were serving out their time, they were regarded as slaves in that they might be bought and sold for their services. You have already read how unjustly they were treated by Governor Samuel Argall. If a servant ran away twice from his master, on being caught, he was branded with the letter "R" to show that he was a runaway or fugitive. In 1619 there was a great demand for servants and slaves because the planters were taking Yeardley's advice, and were raising large crops of tobacco to ship to England. In 1619 twenty thousand pounds of tobacco were shipped; in 1620 forty thousand; in 1622 sixty thousand, and by 1700 more than fifteen million pounds of tobacco were sent annually to England.

The first negro slaves were bought by the planters in order that they might get a class of laborers suited to tobacco culture. Twenty-five years passed, however, before the Virginians began to buy many negroes. Governor Yeardley encouraged* African slavery by buying

* He also encouraged farming in many ways. He caused the planters to sow wheat and to raise Indian corn as well as tobacco. He fertilized the soil with marl and promoted cattle raising. On his own plantation he had a herd of twenty-four cows. He was the first to erect a windmill in Virginia. His estate at his death was estimated at 0,000, a large amount for that time.

eight out of the first twenty. He put them to work on his plantation near Bermuda Hundred. When he died, he directed in his will that his "negars" should be sold.

After two years of faithful service, Yeardley requested the London Company to appoint a successor and he retired from the governorship. He was succeeded by Sir Francis Wyatt, who brought to Virginia a charter confirming Yeardley's action in establishing the House of Burgesses.

In 1622 occurred the terrible Indian massacre. Opechancanough, who had succeeded Powhatan, was disturbed by the growth of the colony, and longed for an opportunity to check it. The immediate cause of trouble was due to an Indian warrior, Nemattenow, who went to the store of a settler named Morgan, enticed him away and murdered him. Two young men, Morgan's servants, killed the Indian in revenge. In order to avenge the death of this warrior, Opechancanough planned an attack on the English settlers. On the twenty-second of March, 1622, at a time when the settlers were totally unprepared, the Indians came upon them in their fields and at their homes, and brutally butchered men, women and children. In three hours' time, three hundred and forty-nine of the settlers had been killed.

Sir George Yeardley, who had made his home in Virginia after he resigned his governorship, was at once made leader of the forces to subdue the Indians. With three hundred men he drove the Indians south of the James or north of the York River, destroying their cabins and settlements and seizing their corn and provisions. The Indians were hunted and killed without quarter. Many were also forced back into the wilderness west of where Richmond now stands, and their favorite hunting grounds and fields were taken away from them.

CHARLES I.

Soon after this, King James, on account of the liberal policy of the London Company, took away its charter, and he himself began to manage the colony (1624). Virginia thus became a royal province, and the governors, from this time to the Revolution, were appointed by the king. James continued Sir Francis Wyatt as governor, until he could prepare a special book of laws for the government of Virginia. Fortunately, perhaps. for Virginia, James died in 1625, without having completed his plans of government for the colony. Charles I. succeeded him as king and reappointed Wyatt as governor of Virginia. The House of Burgesses was continued, so that, after all, Virginia did not lose the liberal government which she had received from the London Company.

In 1625 Wyatt gave up the governorship and returned to his home in Ireland, and Sir George Yeardley was again made governor. This was his third time in office. He remained governor but eighteen months. In November, 1627, he died and was buried at Jamestown. Recently a tomb, in which some knight was buried, has been found within the old church, and it is generally thought to be the grave of Sir George Yeardley.

There were only three hundred and fifty people in the colony when Yeardley first became governor, but at the time of his death there were probably thirty-five hundred or four thousand people, at least a thousand emigrants having come over during his last year as governor. This population was distributed among seventeen or eighteen plantations, most of them along the banks of the James River. Yeardley seems to have been a man well suited to govern the colony, and the affairs of Virginia, whenever they were in his hands,

Published by the courtesy of Mr. R. A. Lancaster, Jr, of Richmond.
EXCAVATIONS IN THE JAMESTOWN CHURCH, SHOWING THE SUP-
POSED TOMB OF YEARDLEY.

prospered. The colonists believed that he was an
honest, upright and virtuous man, and when he died,
the Virginia council in a letter to the English government, praised in the highest terms Yeardley and his
virtues.

Review Questions.

Who was Yeardley? What was the condition of Virginia
when he first became governor? Tell of the beginning of the
cultivation of tobacco. How did the king honor Yeardley?
Tell of the increase in population when Yeardley was
governor for the second time. What was the House of
Burgesses? Describe its first meeting. What were some of
its acts? Tell how wives were brought over for the colonists.
Explain what is meant by indented servants. Tell of the
introduction of negro slaves. Why did the planters want

slaves? Describe the massacre of 1622. What was done to the Indians? Tell of Yeardley's governorship for the third time. Describe the growth of Virginia under Yeardley.

Geography Study.

Map of Virginia.—Locate Bermuda Hundred and Jamestown. How would you go from Bermuda Hundred to Jamestown?

CHAPTER VI.

WILLIAM CLAIBORNE.

1589–1676.

FOR forty years in the early history of the colony of Virginia, a prominent figure was William Claiborne.

WILLIAM CLAIBORNE.

He was born in Westmorelandshire, northern England, of an old English family, and seems to have received a good education. In 1621 he was appointed by the London Company as surveyor of the plantations of Virginia, and arrived at Jamestown along with Sir Francis Wyatt, who came to succeed Governor Yeardley. As surveyor of the colony, Claiborne collected materials for the first reliable map of Virginia. He became prominent in the colony as a member of the council, and acquired a large estate containing more than fifty thousand acres of land. In 1625 Charles I. appointed him Secretary of State for Virginia.

In 1629, Lord Baltimore, a prominent English Catholic, came to Virginia with the view of making it his home; but the people were strong believers in the Church of England and did not desire any Catholics in their midst. They therefore told Lord Baltimore that before he could live in Virginia, he would have to take an oath acknowledging the English king as the head of the Church. Of course Lord Baltimore refused to make such an

THE FIRST LORD BALTIMORE.

oath, because, as a good Catholic, he believed the Pope to be the true head of the Church.

Claiborne was one of those who wished to make his lordship take the oath, and he was active in demanding that Lord Baltimore should leave the colony for refusing to accept the king as the head of the Church. However, in spite of the fact that the officials would not allow Lord Baltimore to settle in Virginia, it seemed that they were not willing for him to be ill-treated while he tarried in the colony. At the time, there was at

Jamestown, one Thomas Tindal, who, because of his hatred for the Catholics, insulted Lord Baltimore, calling him a liar and threatening to knock him down. For this discourtesy Tindal was tried and placed in the pillory for two hours.

Lord Baltimore returned to England and received from King Charles a charter to settle north of the Potomac River, in the territory that had previously been included in the Virginia grant. It was provided that he should take only such land as had not been cultivated. The Virginians did not like this action on the part of King Charles I., and they protested violently against Lord Baltimore's receiving a part of their lands. But their objection was ignored by the king, and Lord Baltimore was allowed to send over a colony of Catholics and such others as cared to join them, and a settlement was made at St. Mary's, Maryland, in 1634.

William Claiborne, acting under license from the king, had formed a partnership in London under the name of Clobery and Company, to trade with the Indians and to make discoveries in Virginia. In 1631 he sent to Kent Island in the Chesapeake Bay, not far from the present site of Annapolis, a band of one hundred settlers. As this island was then considered within the limits of Virginia, Claiborne's colony was allowed to send one representative to the House of Burgesses. In 1632 the colony was represented by Captain Nicholas Martian, who was an ancestor of George Washington.

When Claiborne learned that Lord Baltimore was to make a settlement on the Chesapeake Bay, he appealed to the king to protect him in his right to Kent Island. He claimed that Lord Baltimore's charter was for unsettled lands, and that, since his island was already settled, it was therefore not included in the Maryland grant. So, when the Maryland colony arrived, Claiborne refused to consider his settlement as a part of Lord Baltimore's possessions. He was then accused of trying to stir up the Indians against the Marylanders, but this accusation was shown to be false. Lord Baltimore, however, ordered Leonard Calvert, the governor of Maryland, to proceed to Kent Island to take possession of it, and to make Claiborne a prisoner. On hearing of these instructions of Lord Baltimore, Claiborne again appealed to the king. Charles I. thereupon wrote that Lord Baltimore had no claims on Kent Island, and that his action in trying to get it was "contrary to justice."

A war then broke out between Claiborne's settlement and Maryland. Governor Calvert captured some of Claiborne's boats in Pocomoke Sound and a little later sent an expedition against Kent Island, which was conquered and made part of Maryland. Two of Claiborne's followers were taken to St. Mary's, tried and condemned to be hanged. Though the Maryland government failed to take Claiborne prisoner, it caused

THE DISPUTED TERRITORY.

him to be indicted and convicted of murder and piracy. His personal property on the island was seized and appropriated to Lord Baltimore's use. Having lost his possessions, Claiborne sailed for England, where he brought the whole matter before King Charles I., who referred it to a number of his advisors, known as the "Lords Commissioners of Plantations." Their decision was rendered against Claiborne and in favor of Lord Baltimore.

Not despairing, Claiborne returned to Virginia and tried to recover some of his personal property, but the Maryland government claimed that he had forfeited it. He then settled down to a quiet life in Virginia, and in 1642, Charles I., in order to conciliate him, made him treasurer of Virginia for life.

Claiborne was always popular with the Virginians, and while he was disputing with Lord Baltimore, they had helped and upheld him. Sir John Harvey, then governor of Virginia, had sided with Lord Baltimore, and he deliberately removed Claiborne from the office of Secretary of State for the colony. Partly on this account, but chiefly because he took public funds for his own use, the people, especially in York County,* became greatly incensed with Governor Harvey. A petition was presented to the Council against him, and after considering the case, a meeting of the House of Burgesses was called. The Council and Burgesses thereupon deposed Harvey and sent him to England for trial. This was really a rebellion against Charles I., who declared that Harvey should go back to Virginia if he stayed but a day.

Hardly had Claiborne become treasurer of the colony, before Charles I. was at war with Parliament. Claiborne joined himself to the Puritan or Parliamentary party, though he was a member of the Church of England. Undoubtedly his desire was to get the Puritan support, so that he could recover Kent Island.

About this time, 1644, the Roman Catholic government in Maryland was overthrown by Captain Richard Ingle. Claiborne is thought to have encouraged Cap-

---

* About this time, 1634, the twenty-three plantations in Virginia were divided into eight counties: York, James City, Accomac, Charles City, Elizabeth City, Henrico, Warrick, and Isle of Wight.

tain Ingle, though there is no proof of it. Governor
Calvert fled to Virginia, but the next year returned with
a Virginia force furnished him by Governor Berkeley
and re-established himself in Maryland.

As soon as the Commonwealth was established in
England with Cromwell at its head, Claiborne and
Richard Bennett, with two others, were appointed by
Parliament as commissioners to reduce Virginia and

Maryland, those two
colonies having pro-
claimed Prince
Charles (afterwards,
Charles II.), as their
king. Governor
Berkeley urged the
Virginians to fight,
but an assembly be-
ing called, an ,agree-
ment was reached
with Bennett and
Claiborne whereby

CHARLES II.

the Commonwealth was acknowledged in Virginia, but
the colony was granted free trade, such as the people of
England then enjoyed. Richard Bennett was made
governor of Virginia, and Claiborne became Secretary of
State for the colony and a member of the council (1652).

Maryland was likewise forced to accept the Commonwealth. Governor Stone was removed and the government of the colony was put into the hands of the council. Later the commissioners restored Governor Stone, but as he did not observe the agreement which he made, a civil war broke out in Maryland. The Puritan party, which had the support of Claiborne, met Stone in battle near the mouth of the Severn River. Lord Baltimore's adherents were severely defeated and a number were taken prisoners. Twenty were killed and many were wounded ''and all the place was strewed with papist beads where they fled. Several of the prisoners were condemned to death by court-martial and four of the principals, one of them a councillor, were executed on the spot. Captain William Stone (governor), likewise sentenced, owed his escape to the intercession of some women.'' At once, the Puritan government was established and the Catholics who had settled Maryland, were not allowed to have any voice in the government.

Lord Baltimore appealed to Cromwell to restore his rights. The Virginians at the advice of Claiborne did all in their power to prevent his lordship from again getting control of Maryland, and they showed that Virginia had settled Kent Island before Lord Baltimore's colony came to America. In 1657 the quarrel was settled in favor of Lord Baltimore, and Claiborne had to retire from Maryland, after a contest of twenty-four years.

Claiborne continued as Secretary of State for the colony of Virginia until 1660, at which time he was removed from office by Sir William Berkeley, who again became governor of Virginia. After this he led

CLAIBORNE'S AUTOGRAPH.

the life of a planter, living in New Kent county, which county he had organized and named after Kent Island. In 1660 he was elected a member of that House of Burgesses which Berkeley kept in power for sixteen years. In 1675 he presented a petition to Charles II. in which he showed that in his attempt to settle Kent Island he had lost six thousand pounds ($30,000), and he begged the king that Lord Baltimore might be forced to make restoration for this loss. To this petition, Charles paid no attention. All of Claiborne's friends in England were now dead, and he had no one to help him.

Claiborne died, probably, the next year (1676), in the midst of Bacon's Rebellion, at the age of eighty-seven. He left three sons, from whom many of the best people of our state claim descent.

Claiborne has wrongly been called a "rebel." He did not overthrow the Maryland government, except in carrying out the instructions which he had received from England. He felt that he had been misused, and being a persevering and determined man, he tried for years to get his claims to Kent Island recognized. Surely no man should be called a rebel who demands his just rights.

Review Questions.

What were the different offices which Claiborne held? Tell of Lord Baltimore's trip to Virginia. Tell the story of Thomas Tindal. Why did not Claiborne want Lord Baltimore to settle Maryland? Tell about the struggle over Kent Island. Tell the story of Governor Harvey. Name the first counties of Virginia. What was the Commonwealth in England? On what terms did Virginia accept the Commonwealth? Who was Bennett? What became of Claiborne after the Restoration? Why was Claiborne wrongly called a rebel?

Geography Study.

Map of Virginia and Maryland. Find Annapolis, St. Mary's, Kent Island and Severn River. Locate Jamestown and the counties of New Kent, Charles City, York, James City, Accomac, Elizabeth City, Henrico, Warrick and Isle of Wight.

CHAPTER VII.

WILLIAM BERKELEY.

1600–1677.

AT the time of Governor Yeardley's death, Virginia was in a prosperous condition. Much of this prosperity was lost under the unworthy Governor John Pott, who was removed from office, brought to trial and found guilty of stealing cattle. His successor, Sir John Harvey, caused severe measures to be passed against persons who did not worship God according to the Church of England, which was the established church of Virginia. Harvey, as you may remember, was removed by the Council and Burgesses, and for the few following years Sir Francis Wyatt was for a second time governor of Virginia. In 1642 he was succeeded by Sir William Berkeley, who, with the exception of the Commonwealth period, was governor of Virginia for thirty-five years.

Sir William Berkeley was born in England about 1600. He was a man of fine education, a graduate of Oxford University and afterwards a fellow of Merton College. He was a warm friend of Charles I., who greatly admired him and made him a member of his council. Berkeley was a man of elegant manners, of refinement and culture. In those days, many of the courtiers were literary men, and it is said that Sir William wrote plays which were acted in the London theaters. Though a cultured man, he had narrow views as to the rights of the people, and was a bigot in matters of religion. One of the first acts of his governorship was to insist on a law against those who were not members of the established church. Berkeley was anxious to drive from Virginia the Puritans who had come from New England; so he caused the House of Burgesses to pass a law to the effect that

THE OLD CHURCH AT SMITHFIELD.

"all ministers whatsoever . . . are to be conformable to the orders and constitutions of the Church of England and the laws therein established, and

not otherwise be admitted to teach or preach pub-
licly or privately; and that the governor and council
do take care that all non-conformists . . . shall be
compelled to depart the colony with all convenience."

In 1644 the old Indian chief, Opechancanough, attempted a second massacre of the English on the frontier. Berkeley at once led the forces against him, seized
the old king and brought him a prisoner to Jamestown.
Opechancanough was now over ninety years of age,
and, with paralyzed eyelids, could not see without their
being raised for him. One day, hearing footsteps in
his prison cell, he requested that his eyelids might be
raised; and, when he saw the great crowd that had
come to view him, he sent for the governor. When
Berkeley appeared, the old Indian chief with great
indignation addressed him: "Had it been my fortune
to take Sir William Berkeley prisoner, I would not have
descended to make a show of him." A few weeks after,
Opechancanough was shot by one of his guards.

As you learned in the chapter on Claiborne, King
Charles went to war with the English Parliament. His
followers were chiefly those who held to the English
Church and believed that the king should have unlimited power. They were, as a rule, from the higher
and titled classes of England and were called the Cavaliers. Opposed to Charles was the body of the middle

class that did not accept the Church of England, believing that religion stood greatly in need of purification and that many of the customs and amusements of the Cavaliers should be abolished. They likewise thought that the king should exercise few powers outside of those that Parliament granted him. These people lived very simply, caring little for fashion or dress. The Cavaliers wore their hair long, but the opponents of Charles, regarding this fashion as effeminate, had their hair cropped close to the head and for that reason were called Roundheads. Their great leader was Oliver Cromwell.

Charles was defeated, taken prisoner, condemned as a traitor and executed on the block. Many of his followers fled to Virginia, which thus came to be known as the Cavalier colony.

In 1650 there were in Virginia about fifteen thousand English and three hundred negroes, living in fourteen counties. Many

ROUNDHEAD AND CAVALIER

Puritans had come to the colony, probably more than a thousand, which fact explains why Virginia so readily

surrendered to Bennett and Claiborne, the commissioners of the English Commonwealth.

Berkeley quietly retired from the governorship and
took up his residence at his plantation, Green Springs,
about six miles west of Jamestown. Richard Bennett,
a Puritan who had once been driven out of Virginia

RUINS AT "GREEN SPRINGS."

because he would
not conform to the
English Church, was
elected governor.
Two years later, the
Virginian Assembly
elected Edmund
Diggs to this office,
and his salary was
fixed at twenty
thousand pounds of
tobacco annually.

The next year Thomas Matthew was chosen governor.

In 1658, Cromwell died, and it was generally believed
that the Commonwealth of England, bereft of its leader,
would soon fall. About the same time, Governor
Matthews died, and Sir William Berkeley was elected
governor by the Virginia House of Burgesses. Shortly
afterwards Charles II. was made King of England,
and he at once confirmed the election of Berkeley.

Virginia was now called the Old Dominion, this name, so the story goes, having been given it by Charles II., because he believed that the Virginians had always been loyal to him.

Through Berkeley's influence, the House of Burgesses passed an act against all Quakers in the colony, declaring that they taught lies and would destroy the government. All Quakers were to be sent out of the colony, all vessels bringing them to Virginia were to be fined one hundred pounds of tobacco, and any person entertaining a Quaker would be obliged to pay one hundred pounds sterling ($500).

During the next fifteen years, Berkeley ruled Virginia much as if he had been its king. While the Commonwealth existed, the people had enjoyed much freedom. The House of Burgesses had been elected yearly, and it, in return, had elected the governors. Thus Virginia was as much a free state as it is to-day. On the restoration of Charles II. to the throne of England, a great change took place. A House of Burgesses was elected which was in favor of restricting the liberties of the people. This body was composed of two representatives each from twenty counties and one representative from Jamestown. With them sat the governor and the sixteen councillors of state. Sir William Berkeley continued this assembly, which was composed of his followers, for sixteen years, during which time he would not allow another general election. Well might the liberty-loving Virginians be ready to enter into a rebellion against Berkeley and his tyrannical government! .

In 1671, Berkeley reported the condition of the colony to the Commissioners of Plantations in England. He placed the population of Virginia at forty thousand, of which number two thousand were slaves and six thousand white ("indented") servants. With reference to education he reported that every man, accord-

this 15th daie of May 1672

William Berkeley

BERKELEY'S SIGNATURE TO A DOCUMENT.

ing to his ability, instructed his own children, as was the case in England. There were forty-eight parishes in Virginia, most of them supplied with preachers, but not good ones, since only the worthless ones were sent from England. Berkeley wrote: "Our ministers are well paid and by my consent could be better, if they would pray oftener and preach less." His closing remarks were: "But I thank God there are no free schools and no printing, and I hope we shall not have these hundred years, for learning has brought disobedience and heresy and sects into the world, and printing has divulged them and libels against the best government. God keep us from both." This shows the narrow spirit of the man, and becoming yet more insolent as he grew older, he made himself ever more unpopular. He ruled the colony with an iron hand, expecting that his will should be obeyed as law.

Finally, many of the Virginians, with Nathaniel Bacon as leader, rose in rebellion. With great difficulty Berkeley managed to quell them, and, the rebels once in his power, he showed what a tyrant he was by causing twenty-three of them to suffer death.

In 1677, Charles II. removed Berkeley from the governorship. It is said that when Berkeley reached England, the king refused to see him, declaring: "That old fool (Berkeley) has hung more men in that naked country (Virginia), than I have done for the murder of my father (Charles I.)." From this rebuke Berkeley never recovered, dying soon afterwards of a broken heart.

Review Questions.

Who was John Pott? What law was passed while Harvey was governor? Tell of Berkeley's education and life in England. Tell of the law against Puritans. What did Opechancanough try to do, and what was his fate? Who were the Cavaliers? Who were the Roundheads? Who was Cromwell? What governors were elected by the Burgesses? How

7

did Virginia get the name of Old Dominion? Tell of the law against the Quakers. What was the character of Berkeley's rule from 1660 to 1775 ? Tell of Berkeley's report to England about the condition of Virginia. What did he say about schools and printing ? Tell how he treated some of Bacon's followers. Write a composition on Berkeley's character.

Geography Study.

Map of England.—Find London and Oxford. *Map of Virginia.*—Locate Jamestown. How far is it from Rich-mond ? How far is it from London to Jamestown?

CHAPTER VIII.

NATHANIEL BACON.

1646(?)–1676.

THE leader of the   bellion against Sir William Berkeley and his government was Nathaniel Bacon, Jr. His ather was an English gentleman, Mr. Thomas Bacon, probably a kinsman of Lord Francis Bacon, the English philosopher. Nathaniel Bacon, Jr., was born about 1646 and was educated at Oxford University, England, after which he traveled extensively in Europe. He was a young man of brilliant attainments, and the general opinion was that he would take a leading part in English politics. Before he reached manhood he married a daughter of Sir Edward Duke, greatly angering his father. He seems to have been in need of money; so, deciding to try his fortune in the New World, he came with his wife to Virginia. He soon took a prominent part in the affairs of the colony and was made a member of the governor's council. Brave and daring, he attracted to him many of the younger men of the colony.

When Bacon arrived in Virginia, he found that Berkeley was very distasteful to the majority of the people. Virginia had but one industry, and that was tobacco raising. Upon this many restrictions had been placed by law, and the taxes were so heavy that the profits of tobacco growing were much reduced. In addition to this, the people were dissatisfied because Berkeley insisted on refusing to all except land owners the right to vote, as was done in England. When Berkeley became governor, all freeman in Virginia could vote, but through his influence it became the law that no man could vote unless he owned a landed estate and kept house. Moreover, as before stated, Berkeley did not call an assembly for sixteen years, and thus the masses of the people had no opportunity to influence law-making. But the immediate cause of Bacon's Rebellion was Berkeley's failure to protect the frontier settlements from Indian raids.

The people of Virginia were somewhat superstitious in those days, and just one year before Bacon's uprising there occurred three wonderful things which indicated that something serious would happen in the colony. First of all, a large comet was seen every evening for a week, streaming like a horse's tail across the heavens. The people then believed that a comet indicated war. At the same time, there were flights of pigeons in such flocks that the sky was darkened and limbs of large trees were broken down at night when the pigeons went to roost. The third strange sight was a swarm of "flies," about an inch long and the size of a man's little finger, which came out of the ground and ate all the leaves from the tops of the trees. They were prob-

AN OVERSEER'S HOUSE.

ably locusts, which are said to have the letter "W" on their wings as the sign of war.

In the summer of 1675, the Indians began to kill some of the English settlers in the frontier counties. They murdered an overseer on Bacon's plantation not far from Richmond, and other men were killed on the Rappahannock, York and Pamunkey rivers. These crimes were reported to Governor Berkeley, and he promised to render assistance. But the promised aid did not come, and the people in the stretch of countr▪

from Richmond's present site to West Point on the York River rose for their own defence, choosing Bacon as their leader.   A request was made of the governor that Bacon should be officially appointed to lead them against the Indians.   When the commission failed to come, the people began to murmur, saying that Berkeley was engaged in the fur trade with the Indians and was afraid that his business would be interfered with.

In the meantime, five hundred men had come together and, without commission, at once marched into the wilderness to attack the Indians.   Berkeley immediately proclaimed all men who did not return within a day to be rebels; thereupon, most of the men owning large estates went home, but Bacon, with fifty-seven others, continued in arms.   This small force proceeded against the Indians, and near where Richmond to-day stands, fought a battle in which only three whites were killed though one hundred and fifty Indians were slain.

By the time Bacon reached home, Berkeley had at last decided to issue writs for the election of a new House of Burgesses.   Bacon was selected as a member from Henrico county.   As the time for the meeting of the House of Burgesses approached, he went in his boat down the James River, but, on reaching Jamestown, he was at once arrested by the high sheriff and carried before Governor Berkeley. To Bacon's surprise, Berkeley treated him civilly and allowed him to go free on his word of honor that he would not create a disturbance. The old governor was undoubtedly afraid of the people, or he would not have treated Bacon in this lenient manner. There was great consternation in Jamestown among the Burgesses and people, and on all sides was heard, "All's over; Bacon is taken."

In the Council, there was another Nathaniel Bacon, Berkeley's friend and the "rebel's" cousin. By this relative Bacon was persuaded against his will to offer an

BACON'S AUTOGRAPH.

apology to Governor Berkeley for having proceeded against the Indians without a commision. When the assembly met, the governor rose and said, "If there be 'joy in the presence of angels over one sinner that repenteth,' there is joy now, for we have a penitent sinner come before us." Turning to the sergeant-at-arms, he said, "Call Mr. Bacon." Bacon, appearing, bowed on one knee before the governor, delivered into his hands a paper confessing his crimes, and begged pardon of God, the king and the governor. Berkeley then said, "God forgive you. I forgive you and all that were with you." Though the governor stated that he forgave all, twenty of the men who had gone in arms with Bacon were at that time in prison.

A few days later Jamestown was astir. The report was abroad, "Bacon is fled: Bacon is fled!" Berkeley had made promises to Bacon which he was unwilling to keep, and it was rumored that even attempts were to be made upon the life of the young rebel. Bacon went up the river, raised a force of about four hundred men and after four days led them into Jamestown to demand by force a commission allowing them to fight the Indians. Berkeley at first refused, and, when Bacon's troops surrounded the capitol building, shouting, "We'll have it! We'll have it!" the governor was greatly incensed. He came out of the capitol, and, baring his breast before Bacon and his men, said, "Here, shoot me! 'Fore God, fair mark, shoot!"

From the painting by Kelley.

BACON DEMANDING HIS COMMISSION.

To this Bacon replied, "No, may it please your honor, we will not hurt a hair of your head, or any other man's. We are come for a commission to save our lives from the Indians, which you have so often promised, and now we will have it before we go."

At last, the governor signed the commission appointing Bacon general of the forces to be raised against the Indians. Hardly had Bacon started for the forests with about a thousand men, before Berkeley proclaimed Bacon a rebel and traitor and collected an army of twelve hundred men to seize him. Hearing of Berkeley's action, Bacon turned back to meet him, but the governor, finding himself deserted by all but a few hundred of his men, sailed away to Accomac, and Bacon again proceeded against the Indians.

While the young leader was fighting the savages in the wilderness, Berkeley returned and fortified Jamestown. Besides the capitol building and a church, Jamestown at that time contained some sixteen or eighteen houses, most of them built of brick but not all occupied, since there were not more than a dozen families on the island. The inhabitants of the place made their living chiefly by keeping boarding-houses for the Burgesses and state officials who had to live at the capitol.

The town was very easy to defend, but Bacon succeeded in taking it by an act which certainly was lacking in gallantry. He sent soldiers through the neighboring community to bring to his camp some six or eight ladies whose husbands were with Berkeley in the town. One of these was sent to inform her husband and the other followers of Berkeley that Bacon would place the ladies in front of his men if Berkeley should make a sally from the town. With these ladies to protect his troops Bacon completed his entrenchments and Berkeley's soldiers did not dare to fire for fear that they might hurt the women. One attempt, however, was made to drive Bacon back, and when this failed, Berkeley again sailed away to Accomac. Bacon then captured Jamestown and burned the place.*

Shortly after this, Bacon went into Gloucester county, where the people, he had heard, were in sympathy with Berkeley. As a test of their allegiance, he called upon them to take an oath against Berkeley, and many complied with this request. While in Gloucester, he was taken ill at the house of a friend, Mr. Pate, and here he died, the first day of October, 1676. His enemies

* In August, 1676, Bacon had called a meeting of the people at Middle Plantation, now Williamsburg. Here his followers took an oath that they would fight with him against Berkeley and the Indians. Bacon addressed his men in an eloquent speech advocating opposition to the English government if it should send aid to Berkeley. Among those who took the oath were many of the leading citizens of the colony.

spread it abroad that he was an excessive drinker and that his death was due to this cause; but this report was, beyond a doubt, false, and Bacon died probably from fever.

According to all accounts, Bacon was a young man of great native gifts and wide culture. He was a very persuasive and impressive orator, and had the reputation of being able to speak more "sense in a few words" than any other man in the colony.

With Bacon's death, ended the rebellion. Berkeley soon secured control of the places which Bacon had seized and caused some twenty-three of the latter's followers to be put to death. When William Drummond, one of Bacon's commanders, was captured and brought before Berkeley, the hard-hearted old tyrant said: "Mr. Drummond, you are very welcome. I am more glad to see you than any man in Virginia. Mr. Drummond, you shall be hanged in half an hour," and it is reported that the sentence was actually carried out inside of two hours.

A very touching story is told about Major Cheesman, another of Bacon's men. It is said that when the major was brought before the governor, he was asked why he had joined Bacon's Rebellion, and, before he could make a reply, his wife came in and bowed before Governor Berkeley. She declared that she had urged her husband to fight with Bacon, and tl but for her influence he would not have joined rebellion.   Upon her bended knees, she begged William to hang her instead of her husband. ·' governor, furious with her, called her by an insult name and ordered her husband to be thrown into pri where he soon died from bad treatment.

Bacon's Rebellion was the first open attempt at erty; it was a war against English tyranny as exerci by a colonial governor.   It took place just a cent before the Revolution, and when we think proudl Washington, who, at the head of our armies, won fo our independence from England, we should not fo the first rebel, Bacon, who one hundred years be had struck the first blow for liberty.

Review Questions.

Tell of Bacon before he came to Virginia.   How w received in Virginia?   What were the causes of Ba Rebellion?   Tell of the three wonderful natural occurrei Why did Bacon wish to go against the Indians?   Why Berkeley refuse to give the commission?   Why did he claim Bacon a rebel?   Tell of Bacon's arrest and pai Why did Bacon flee from Jamestown?   Tell of his re and his commission.   What kind of place was Jamest Tell of Bacon's capture of Jamestown.   Tell of Bacon's L Tell of his death.   Give an account of Berkeley's treat of Drummond and Cheesman.   Why should we reme Bacon?

Geography Study.

Map of Virginia.—Locate Jamestown, Richmond, Wil-
lamsburg, West Point, the York, Rappahannock and Pamun-
rivers, Accomac county and Gloucester county.   How far
from Richmond to Accomac county? How would you
from Jamestown to Accomac county?

CHAPTER IX.

JAMES BLAIR.

1655–1743.

At the close of Bacon's Rebellion, Virginia settled down to a quiet life. The main political events from that time to the Revolution were the contests between the governors and the colonists. As a rule, the governors were English gentlemen who were in need of money, and had come to Virginia to get rich, after which they hoped to return home and live in great state. The Virginians did not close their eyes to the greed of the governors, and time and again the House of Burgesses blocked measures which the governors were trying to carry in order that they might gain wealth. The Burgesses often refused to give a governor a fixed salary, and in this way held him in check. In the constant clash between the governors on the one side, and the people on the other, many a statesman was being trained to fight for liberty and independence.

Virginia grew in population and resources. About 1685 there were twenty counties. The population was

t sixty thousand, containing six thousand negro
s. The only crop for export was tobacco. This
d a misfortune for the colonists, for tobacco
their money, and when there was an unusually

crop, its ex-
ge value naturally
eased. On the
hand, if the crop
small, there was
suffering. Under
Culpeper, who was
nor from 1680 to
there was much
tisfaction among
people because of
heavy taxes and
ctions on the ex-
ing of tobacco.
planters were re-

LORD CULPEPER.

d to send their tobacco from certain ports
; the rivers, at which ports a tax of two shillings
hogshead was levied on all the tobacco shipped.
caused considerable inconvenience to many
ers, as they were obliged to go to a great deal
ouble to load their crops, which had before been
on vessels at the planters' own wharves. For these

reasons, the tobacco growers decided to resist the government; not with armed forces, however, but by making an agreement among themselves to cut down their tobacco plants and thus to reduce the shipments to England. This was called the "Tobacco Insurrection," and many crops of tobacco were destroyed, chiefly in Gloucester county. Culpeper caused many planters to be arrested and thrown into jail, and six men were actually hanged because they were plant cutters.

From 1685 to 1743, Virginia had about twelve governors, who were constantly quarreling with the people. During these fifty-eight years, the chief opponent of the governors was James Blair, a native of Scotland. He was a man of good education, having been graduated from the University of Edinburgh with the degree of Master of Arts. He became a minister of the Episcopal Church, after which he moved into England where he met Doctor Compton, Bishop of London. The Bishop was greatly pleased with young Blair, whom he found an energetic and zealous man, and soon spoke to him of the great need of good preachers in Virginia and urged him to go to that colony. At that time there were few good ministers who were willing to go to Virginia. When Blair saw the great opportunity which offered itself in the New World, he agreed to leave England; and accordingly, in 1685, he landed in Virginia. At first he took charge of the church in Henrico County, but later he became the pastor at Jamestown and in 1710 he accepted the charge of Bruton-Parish Church in Williamsburg,

BRUTON—PARISH CHURCH.

where he remained until his death in 1743. In four years after he had reached Virginia, the Bishop of London made him his representative in the colony, and he held this position for fifty years.

In Virginia, Church and State were connected, which meant that there was a church supported and upheld by the government of the colony. The established church was the Church of England, known as the Episcopal Church. The governor was the head of the colonial church, just as the king was the head of the church in England. Virginia had no bishop, but since the colony

8

had been settled by a company with headquarters in London, the Bishop of London was regarded as the chief church official in Virginia. Of course, he never came to the colony, but sent a representative, called a commissary; this title Blair held for fifty years.

As commissary, he could not ordain ministers, so that if any Virginian desired to take orders, he had to go to England for ordination by the Bishop. The duties of the commissary consisted in visiting the parishes and correcting the clergy in their mode of life. He could not remove a minister or put one in charge of a parish, for these were powers which belonged to the governor as head of the church. All the people in the colony were taxed to support the church and the ministers received an annual salary, fixed by law, in 1696, at sixteen thousand pounds of tobacco ($640).

When Blair became commissary, the colony was in a low moral condition. Many of the clergy used profane language and were often seen intoxicated. With such clergy Commissary Blair had great difficulty to advance the cause of religion, but by a determined effort he greatly bettered the morals of the church during his half a century of service. At the time of his arrival in Virginia, there were fifty parishes, of which only twenty-two were supplied with ministers. Blair set himself to work to improve the ministry and to fill the twenty-eight vacant parishes. In this cause he labored so zealously that at the time of his death there were only two vacant churches in the colony.

While Blair was at the head of the church, other religious sects were coming to Virginia. In 1710 there were two Presbyterian churches and one Quaker meeting house, and just before the death of Blair, many Scotch-Irish Presbyterians settled the Valley of Virginia. They were allowed to hold services according to their own belief, though all persons were to be taxed to maintain the established church.

Blair exercised influence not only upon the religious matters but upon the political affairs of the colony. He dearly loved Virginia, and put forth his best efforts for her welfare. For a long time he was a member of the council of Virginia, and finally became its president. In the latter position it was his duty to act as governor during the absence from the colony of the king's representative. As commissary and member of the council, he wielded great power, and it was chiefly through his efforts that three governors were removed from office.

The first governor to arouse the wrath of Blair was Andros. This governor had removed Blair from the council on the grounds that a Scotchman was not eligible to membership in that body. Blair thereupon went to England, where he accused the governor of being an enemy to the church, because Andros had made no attempt to fill the vacant parishes. Blair presented his charges so strongly that the Engilsh Board of Trade, which represented the king, removed Andros in 1697.

The next governor to contend with Blair was Sir Francis Nicholson. At first the governor and the commissary were warm friends, but Nicholson soon showed his disagreeable nature and became a tyrannical governor, refusing to listen to Blair with reference to the clergy, or to the council with reference to the affairs of Virginia. Nicholson was such a hot-headed man that he often spoke of the members of the council as rogues, villains and cowards.

The trouble that brought on the final breach between Blair and Nicholson was a love affair. Nicholson had fallen passionately in love with a daughter of Major Lewis Burwell. "It completely upset what little reason there was in Governor Nicholson." He demanded from Major Burwell the hand of his daughter with as much air and presumption as the king of England would have done, but the major refused his consent. Nicholson lost all self-control and swore to Blair that "if the girl married some other man, he would cut the throat of three men: the bridegroom, the minister, and the justice who issued the license." Finally Nicholson concluded that James Blair's brother, Archibald, was his rival, so one day he sent for Dr. Blair and said, "Sir, your brother is a villain and you have betrayed me. Mr. Blair, take notice; I vow to the eternal God that I will be revenged on you and all your family." It is said that Nicholson went so far as to distribute pistols to the students of William and Mary College with the instruction that they should shoot Dr. Blair, their president. Blair went to England, brought charges against Nicholson and had him removed from office (1705).

A third governor made to feel the strength of Blair was Alexander Spotswood, who determined to appoint ministers without consulting the vestrymen in the parishes. Blair complained bitterly and the Virginia clergy were called to consider the case. They decided in favor of Spotswood, but Blair would not yield. He went to England and accused Spotswood, not only of assuming too many rights in connection with church affairs, but of trying to destroy the power of the council in Virginia. Spotswood replied by stating that Blair allowed the churches to go without ministers and even appointed laymen to read the services, though preachers could be secured. Spotswood had such strong support, that at one time it looked as if he would defeat the old commissary, but the people stood behind Blair, and the Board of Trade removed Spotswood (1722). Thus three

governors were forced to lay down the reins of government through Blair's influence.

Blair's great work, however, was the e tablishment of
a college. When he came to Virginia, there were no public schools, and every large planter had his children taught
by a tutor. Sir William Berkeley, as you remember, had
written with delight that there was in his time no free
school in Virginia. An attempt had been made in 1619
to establish a college at Henrico, but the Indian massacre of 1622 prevented the enterprise from becoming
a success. In 1690, when Blair set to work to build a
college, there was no college in America except Har-
vard. Blair's idea was to found a college where men
could be educated for the ministry, because he knew
that Virginia would never have better preachers unless
some were trained in the colony. He also had in mind
the educating and Christianizing of the Indians.* Still
another object in establishing a college was to educate
the young men of Virginia, many of whom could not
go to England for an education, though some went to
Oxford and Cambridge universities.   .

Blair's task was a difficult one. At first the people
and the House of Burgesses would not listen to him,

* One purpose named in the charter of King James of 1606 was to
Christianize the Indians, and from time to time throughout colonial
history certain ministers preached to the Indians. Blair believed that
the best way to make Christians of the Indians was to educate them.

but finally the latter body addressed a petition to William and Mary, the sovereigns of England, asking that a college be established in the colony. Blair went to England to secure a charter and to raise the money necessary to put up a building. England was in the midst of a great war with France, and the leading men would not hear Blair, but still he persevered. He called on the queen, who welcomed him and approved of his plan, and later he got an audience with the king. He pleaded his cause in such a manly and sincere way that King William said to him, "Sir, I am glad that the colony

A VIEW OF THE COLLEGE OF WILLIAM AND MARY.

is upon so good a design, and I will promote it to the best of my power." The king and queen gave him about two thousand pounds ($10,000) in money. The college was endowed with twenty thousand acres of land on the Pamunkey River, and a tax of one cent a pound was levied on all tobacco shipped from Virginia and Maryland to the other colonies. On February 19, 1693, the royal charter was granted, and in honor of the sovereigns the college was called, "William and Mary."

In England opposition soon arose to the use of any of the king's revenue for a college. When Blair went with King William's order to Attorney-General Seymour for the charter, he was asked what was the need of a college in Virginia. Blair replied that there were souls to be saved in Virginia as well as in England, and that the college was to educate men for the ministry. Seymour replied that the colonists did not need to give their time to saving souls, but to making tobacco. This answer showed that the people of England looked on Virginia only as a country where tobacco was to be raised to enrich the English merchants and to bring in a revenue to the English government.

Blair returned to Virginia with his charter, and it was decided to build the college at Middle Plantation, to which the name of Williamsburg was given about this time.*

---

* Jamestown was regarded as a very unhealthful place, and at that time contained only four or five inhabited houses. About five years after the college was established at Williamsburg, the capitol was removed from Jamestown to Williamsburg. Francis Nicholson was then governor of the colony.

Blair was selected president of the institution, and remained in this position for fifty years. The first college building was designed by Sir Christopher Wren, the architect of St. Paul's Cathedral in London.

The first commencement of the college was held in 1700, "at which there was a great concourse of people. Several planters came thither in coaches and others in sloops from New York, Pennsylvania and Maryland, it being a new thing in

From a painting by Kneller.

SIR CHRISTOPHER WREN.

that part of America to hear graduates perform their exercises. The Indians themselves had curiosity, some of them, to visit Williamsburg on that occasion, and the whole country rejoiced, as if they had some relish of learning." Four years later the college building was destroyed by fire; but Blair bravely worked on till the college was rebuilt. Later, from the halls of this college went forth many great statesmen, among whom were Jefferson, Marshall, Monroe and Tyler.

Blair died on April 18th, 1744, being eighty-eight years of age. To the college he willed his library and five hundred pounds ($2,500). He was buried at Jamestown and in the long Latin inscription upon his tombstone, it was said: "He had a handsome person and in the family circle blended cheerfulness with piety. He was a generous friend to the poor and was prompt in lending assistance to all who needed it. He was a liberal benefactor of the college during his life and at his death bequeathed to it his library with the hope that his books, which were mostly religious, might lead the student to those things which lead to salvation."

Review Questions.

What were the main political events in Virginia from Bacon's Rebellion to the Revolution? What was the size of Virginia in 1685? Tell of Culpeper and the Tobacco Insurrection. Tell of Blair's life before he came to Virginia. What was the relation of Church and State in Virginia? Why was Blair called commissary? Tell how Blair improved the religious condition of the colony. Tell of his controversy with Governor Andros. What kind of man was Nicholson? Why was he removed from the governorship? Tell of Blair's quarrel with Spotswood and its results. Why did Blair want a college in Virginia? Tell how he succeeded in establishing one. Tell of Blair's will.

Geography Study.

Map of Scotland.—Find Edinburgh.—*Map of Virginia.* Locate Henrico county and Williamsburg. What counties lie between the James and York rivers?

CHAPTER X.

ALEXANDER SPOTSWOOD.

1676–1740.

n *old painting.*

ALEXANDER SPOTSWOOD.

IN the early part of the eighteenth century, the Earl of Orkney was appointed governor of Virginia, which position he held for nearly forty years; but since he never came to the colony he was represented by a deputy who he title of lieutenant-governor. His most promi-representative was Alexander Spotswood. tswood was born in 1676, at Tangier in Northern

Africa. His father, Robert Spotswood, a physician to
the governor and garrison of Tangier, was of a prominent Scotch family. From his childhood Alexander was
familiar with military life. Entering the English army,
he rose from an ensign through the various offices until
he became a lieutenant-colonel. He served under the
great Duke of Marlborough at the battle of Blenheim,
in Germany, and was there wounded. He came to
Virginia in 1710, and was lieutenant-governor for twelve
years.

Spotswood was a man of considerable learning, and
had a good library and some fine mathematical instruments, which he left at his death to William and Mary
College. He also aided Blair in raising the money to rebuild William and Mary College (which, as you know,
was burned several years before he came to Virginia)
and secured from the college a grant from the House of
Burgesses for one thousand pounds ($5,000). Like
Blair he desired to educate the Indians, and for this purpose he erected a school at Fort Christanna on the
south side of the Meherrin River in what is now Bruns-
wick county. This fort was surrounded by palisades
and in the enclosure were five houses, each of which was
defended by one cannon. The Rev. Charles Griffin was
appointed to conduct this school, and in 1715 there were
seventy-seven Indians under his care. One of the old

cannon from Fort Christanna is still in existence and is preserved on the campus of William and Mary College.

A story is told of a trip which Governor Spotswood made to Christanna. The Indians of that section, called Saponeys, numbered about two hundred. They were under the government of twelve old men. When Spotswood was on a visit to the Fort these old men met him, and laying several skins at his feet, bowed themselves to the ground. They informed the governor that fifteen of their young men had been killed by some Indians called the Genitoes, and secured the governor's permission to go against these Indians and kill fifteen warriors in retaliation. "Sixty young men next made their appearance with feathers in their hair and run through their ears, their faces painted in blue and vermillion, their hair cut in fantastic forms, some looking like cocks' comb, and they had blue and red blankets wrapped around them. This was their war dress, and it made them look like furies. Next came the young women, with long straight black hair reaching down to the waist, with a blanket tied around them and hanging down like a petticoat . . . These Indians greased their bodies and heads with bear's oil, which, with the smoke of their cabins, gave them a disagreeable odor. They looked wild and were mighty shy of an Englishman."

At the time of Spotswood's arrival in Virginia, there

were twenty-five counties containing a population of about seventy-two thousand whites and about twenty-three thousand negroes. Williamsburg was the capital. It was a long town; its main street was called the Duke of Gloucester Street. At one end was situated William and Mary College, and at the other end, three-quarters of a mile distant, was the old capitol, where the General Assembly met from time to time to deliberate upon the affairs of the colony.

The country was not in a prosperous condition. All along the coast were bands of pillaging pirates. As the price of tobacco, the main product, had greatly declined, the colony was seriously hampered in its resources.

Although Spotswood's arrival in Virginia was greeted with joy, in a little while he and the House of Burgesses were quarreling. He wanted the General Assembly to raise heavy taxes to provide better defences for the colony against Indians and pirates. Moreover, his desire was to educate the Indians at William and Mary College. For such purposes money was needed, and the members of the House of Burgesses did not readily vote it, for they were anxious to be relieved from all connection with the Indians, and preferred to drive them into the western lands.

Spotswood also complained that the Burgesses were

men of "mean understanding" and without any public spirit. In writing to the Board of Trade, he stated that on account of the ignorance of the Burgesses none of their committees had a chairman who could "spell English or write common sense." In his opinion this state of affairs was due to the fact that so many unworthy persons had the right to vote, and that they elected men

THE AUTOGRAPH OF SPOTSWOOD.

of their own class. A man who had so much as half an acre of land could vote. On Spotswood's representation, the Board of Trade instructed him to use his influence to raise the qualifications of a voter so that no man could vote unless he had a good landed estate. On one occasion, in making a speech dissolving the House of Burgesses, Spotswood said: "The true interest of your country is not what you have troubled your heads about." Believing that the Burgesses were trying to please the "ignorant population," he said, 'If you have excused yourselves to them, you matter not how you stand before God, your prince or judicious men, or before any others to whom you think you owe not your elections."

We are not to take Governor Spotswood at his word, for he was an old soldier, and wished everything done with military regularity. He did not understand Vir-

ginia conditions so well as the people who lived there—
a fault common to all the English governors. Finding
that the Burgesses would not obey him as did the soldiers, whom he had commanded in the field, and that he
had no power to force them to obedience, he spent his
anger in abusing them.

When Spotswood became governor of Virginia, few
settlements had been made outside of the Tidewater
region. Generally speaking, a line drawn from Alexandria, through Fredericksburg, Richmond and Petersburg, to North Carolina, marked the western limit of
the occupation of Virginia by the English. Some
pioneers, however, had pushed into the wilderness and
settled there, while others had explored to the foot of
the Blue Ridge Mountains, but so far as we know, none
of the Virginians had crossed the Blue Ridge and looked
into the beautiful valley which lies between that ridge
and the rugged Alleghanies.

About the first of August, 1716, Governor Spotswood
determined to cross the Blue Ridge. With some members of his staff he left Williamsburg and drove in his
coach to Germanna, near Fredericksburg. Here he left
his coach and with other gentlemen who joined him,
proceeded on horse along the Rappahannock River,
and in thirty-six days from the time he left Williamsburg, he scaled the mountains near Swift Run Gap.

The company descended the mountains on the west side and reached the Shenandoah River. "Proceeding by the river, they found a place where it is fordable, crossed it, and there on the western bank, the governor formally took possession for King George I. of England. After eight weeks, he returned to Williamsburg, having traveled in all four hundred and forty miles."

GOVERNOR SPOTSWOOD AND THE KNIGHTS OF THE GOLDEN HORSESHOE
CROSSING THE BLUE RIDGE.

It is hard for us to believe that less than two hundred years ago, when Spotswood entered the beautiful valley of Virginia, it was the haunt of bears, wolves, panthers, wild cats and buffaloes. The Indians did not live there, but preserved it for their hunting grounds. Those

9

who accompanied Spotswood on the famous expedition have been known in history as the Knights of the Golden Horseshoe.   At that time in eastern Virginia, on account of the sandy soil, few horseshoes were used; but, when Spotswood and his expedition set out from Fredericksburg over the rocky, untraveled wilderness, it was found necessary that the horses should be shod.   Upon the return from his journey, the governor presented "each of his companions with a golden horseshoe, . . . covered with valuable stones resembling heads of nails with the inscription on one side, 'Sic juvat transcendere montes.'"* The climbing of the mountains was regarded in those days as a dangerous and wonderful undertaking, and it was noised abroad throughout the colony.

In this expedition was an ensign in the British army, John Fontaine, who wrote an account of the trip.   After telling of crossing the Shenandoah River, he said, "It is very deep.   The main course of the water is north. It is four score yards wide in the narrowest part.   We drank some health on the other side and returned, after which I went a swimming in it. . . . I got some grasshoppers and fish, and another and I, we catched a dish of fish, some perch, and a kind of fish they call chub.

* This Latin inscription means : "Thus it delights to cross the mountains."

The others went a hunting and killed deer and turkeys. . . . I graved my name on a tree by the river side, and the governor buried a bottle with a paper enclosed on which he writ that he took possession of this place in the name and for King George I. of England."

All of this great valley including the country between Fredericksburg and the mountains was made a part of Essex county, but four years later it was organized as the county of Spotsylvania (Spotswood-land), named in honor of the governor. Glowing reports of this country were circulated and in a few years settlers were entering the valley. Forty thousand acres of land near where Winchester now stands were granted by Governor Gooch in 1730 to two Pennsylvania brothers, John and Isaac Van Meter. Their grant was bought by another Pennsylvanian, Joyst Hite, who removed his family to Virginia in 1732, and fixed his residence a few miles south of the present town of Winchester. Hite is generally believed to have been the first white man to settle in the valley. In a few years came many Scotch-Irish Presbyterians, a splendid body of settlers,. who made the valley one of the most prosperous parts of Virginia.

In spite of Spotswood's trouble with the House of Burgesses and Commissary Blair, he made a good governor. He put down piracy in the Chesapeake Bay

and in Albemarle Sound, North Carolina. Spotswood
sent an expedition against the pirate John Teach,
known as Blackbeard. The pirate's vessel was discovered in Pamlico Sound, North Carolina, where a
battle was fought. Blackbeard had instructed his

From an old print.

THE OLD CAPITOL AT WILLIAMSBURG.

men to blow up the vessel by putting a match to the
powder magazine if it were discovered that his ship
was going to be captured. Before this order could be
carried out, his ship was boarded, and Blackbeard with
many of his followers was killed.

When Spotswood was removed from the governorship, he went to Germanna, where he had planted a settlement of German Protestants. Sometime before this,
he had obtained for himself grants of land in what is
now Spotsylvania, Orange and Culpeper counties, num-

bering in all about eighty-five thousand acres of land. Upon his tract in Spotsylvania he discovered iron ore, which he began to work. Spotswood was the first person to establish a regular furnace in North America. He had four furnaces at Germanna, from which he sent iron to Great Britain. Spotswood also established an air furnace at Massaponnax in Spotsylvania county, where he made stove backs, andirons and other useful things. Colonel William Byrd called Spotswood the "Tubal Cain of Virginia," after the first man whom the Bible mentions as having worked in iron.

In 1730, Spotswood was made deputy-postmaster for the colonies and he it was who appointed Benjamin Franklin as postmaster for the Province of Pennsylvania. Soon after this he was knighted; and in 1740 he was appointed a major-general in the English army to command troops in an attack upon Carthagena in South America. He joined his troops at Annapolis, Maryland, and was about to sail, when he died on the seventh of June, 1740. It is probable that he lies buried in Annapolis, though it has been claimed by some that his body was brought to Virginia and buried at Yorktown.

There are many prominent families in Virginia that claim descent from Governor Spotswood. His name will always be remembered as the first English man to cross the Blue Ridge Mountains, and to develop the iron industry. The twelve years of his governorship were full of energy, and much was done for the betterment of the colony.

Review Questions.

Who was the Earl of Orkney? Tell of Spotswood's early life. How did he help learning? Tell about the Indian school at Fort Christanna. Describe the Indians. Tell of the size of the colony. What kind of town was Williamsburg? What was Spotswood's opinion of the House of Burgesses? Where were all the settlements in 1720? Describe Spotswood's journey across the Blue Ridge. Tell what Fontaine said of his experience. Who were the Knights of the Golden Horseshoe? Who were the first settlers in the Valley? How did Spotswood treat the pirates? Why was Spotswood called the "Tubal Cain of Virginia?" Tell of his death? What kind of man was he?

Geography Study.

Map of Africa.—Find Tangier. *Map of Virginia.*—Find Southampton county, Alexandria, Fredericksburg, Richmond, Petersburg, Winchester, Orange county, Essex county, Spotsylvania county, Culpeper county, Swift Run Gap and the Shenandoah River. Trace the Blue Ridge and Alleghany Mountains.

CHAPTER XI.

WILLIAM BYRD, JR.

1674–1744.

MUCH has been said about the grandeur of colonial life. On account of the easy acquisition of land and of the growth of the institution of slavery, the Virginia planter was enabled to lead a life of freedom and hospitality.

As a rule, the plantations contained not less than one thousand acres of land, and many planters had much larger estates. On every estate was the mansion house, which was usually built of wood, but sometimes of brick. The first brick houses were constructed about the time that Sir William Berkeley be-

A COLONIAL CHAIR.

came governor. The houses contained from four to six rooms. Governor Berkeley's brick mansion at Green Springs had six rooms, while William Fitzhugh's home in Northern Neck, between the Rappahannock and

Potomac rivers, contained thirteen rooms. For a long time the windows of most of the houses had no glass, but were only lattice panels. The rich planters, however, ordered glass from England. The rooms were heated with great fireplaces guarded by fenders of brass. The furniture was plain, and the bedsteads were tall and large, surrounded by curtains. The tableware consisted of plates of earthenware, sometimes of wood, but more frequently of pewter.

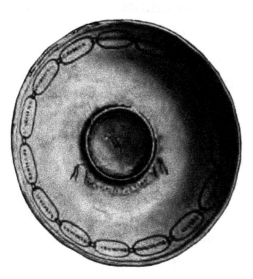

A PLATE OF THE REVOLUTIONARY PERIOD, WHICH BELONGED TO MRS. WASHINGTON.

China, and silver spoons and forks, imported from England, were found only in the homes of the wealthy.

The men wore clothes made of velvets and serge, blue, red, yellow and green being favorite colors. Their trousers came only to the knee, and their stockings were of silk, worsted or cotton. Their shoes were usually low quarters with buckles of brass, steel or silver. Boots were in common use, as they protected the legs in riding, and most of the planters lived constantly on horseback.

The men wore wigs, and had tall caps or hats often in the shape of steeples. The coats of the well-dressed were trimmed with lace, and had buttons of pewter or silver.

The wives of the wealthy planters dressed handsomely, quite as magnificently as the women of high social standing in England. Many of the dresses were made of a flowered silk and were trimmed with lace. The usual costume of a well-dressed woman was a handsome silk gown with silk petticoat of the same color, green silk stockings, a bonnet trimmed with lace, and thread gloves. Around the neck was worn a scarf of many colors. Pearl necklaces, gold and silver earrings, bracelets and finger rings were the kinds of jewelry in general use.

Virginia hospitality in colonial days consisted of great abundance, rather than of great variety. Beef, mutton and pork were the chief meats. A decanter of whiskey or wine always sat on the sideboard, and every large planter had a well-filled wine cellar. We read of one gentleman who ordered at one time twelve hundred gallons of rum. Probably the most popular drink in Virginia was apple cider. Drunkenness was the chief vice in colonial days, and many laws were passed against it. But the laws applied to the middle-class, rather than to the well-to-do, for though the prominent planters drank freely, they were not drunkards.

The chief amusements were cock-fighting, fox-hunting and horse-racing. Frequently great balls were given, and they were attended by planters from long distances. The center of social life was Williamsburg, and the governor was the leader in the social events. All the great planters with their wives and daughters looked with delight to the time when they might attend a ball at the governor's palace.

KING CARTER.

The personal property of a wealthy planter was worth in our money from three to five thousand dollars, while his real estate was worth from twenty thousand to one hundred and fifty thousand dollars. It is probable that the estate of William Byrd, Jr., was worth as much as three hundred thousand dollars. Robert Beverley's property was estimated at two hundred and fifty thousand dollars; and in 1725, there were probably one hundred planters in Virginia who were worth more than fifty thousand dollars. Robert Carter, known as King Carter, owned over three hundred thousand acres of land, and had at the time of his death fifty thousand dollars in money. He also owned twelve hundred slaves. Before 1700 the slave population was comparatively small, but by 1740, in a population of about one hundred and twenty thousand, there were as many as forty thousand slaves.

Among the best-known planters of the early part of the eighteenth century was William Byrd, who lived in Charles City county at the magnificent estate known as Westover. Byrd was born in Virginia in 1674. Before he was ten years of age he was sent for his education to England, where he remained until he was twenty-two years old. He also studied in Holland and France, but most of the time he lived in London, where he studied law and was admitted to the bar. In 1696 he came back to Virginia, and was elected a member of the House of Burgesses from Henrico county. He again went to England to represent Governor Andros in his answer to the charges of Commissary Blair, but he was no match for Blair, and lost his case. A little later he was elected by the Virginia House of Burgesses at the salary of one hundred pounds ($500), as the agent of the colony in London. While living in London he led a life of gayety and became acquainted with many of the literary men of England.   At this time, through the influence of his friend, Sir Robert Southwell, Presi-

EVELYN BYRD, DAUGHTER OF COLONEL BYRD.

dent of the Royal Society, Byrd was made a fellow of that body. He was the first American to receive this distinction. Byrd's love for literature and learning caused him to collect a magnificent library containing more than four thousand volumes.

On the death of his father in 1704, Byrd returned to Virginia.

By his father's will, he was sole heir of the large estates, and he at once took possession of them.   In 1708 he was appointed by Queen Anne a member of the council, which position he held till his death.   He was president of the council for one year, after the death of Blair, and at one time was receiver-general of the colony.

Governor Spotswood, on coming to Virginia, desired

to have absolute charge of the affairs of the colony. Byrd, as receiver-general, looked after the collecting of the king's revenues, and the system in use was not satisfactory to Spotswood.

Thus Spotswood and Byrd were brought into a dispute which was referred to the Board of Trade in London. About this time, Byrd, having gone to England on private business, had the opportunity of pleading his cause before the Board of Trade, which at first was favorable to his side, but soon began

COLONEL WILLIAM BYRD, JR.

to lean toward Spotswood. The governor, feeling that he was the victor, asked that Byrd and also his friends, Commissary Blair and Philip Ludwell, be removed from the council. The board declined to remove these gentlemen, though Byrd had to promise to make peace with the governor. After five years' absence, Byrd returned to Virginia in 1720, and at once he and the other members of the council made friends with Spotswood and agreed to bury the past. The same year Byrd returned to England as agent of the House of Burgesses, and was absent from the colony for another five years. On arriving in Virginia in 1726, he resumed his seat in the Council, and spent the rest of his life in the colony, taking a deep interest in its affairs.

In 1727 Byrd was one of the commissioners to run the dividing line between Virginia and North Carolina, and as a result of his experiences, he wrote a charming book, which you should read. Soon after this he wrote another book called "The Journey to the Land of Eden."*

In his later years, Byrd devoted his time entirely to his plantation. He experimented with new varieties of fruit and studied the medical properties of many plants. To the twenty-six thousand acres of land which he inherited from his father he gradually

---

* About the time that Byrd was writing, the *Virginia Gazette*, the first newspaper in Virginia, was published. The enterprise was begun at the suggestion of several gentlemen, of whom Byrd was probably one. In the edition of 1736 occurred a notice of a play at the theater, and the following notice of the college: "The president, masters and scholars of William and Mary College went, according to their annual custom, in a body to the Governor's to present his Honor with two copies of Latin verses. The president delivered the verses to his Honor, and two of the young men spoke them. It is further observed there were upwards of sixty scholars present; a much greater number than has been any year before since the foundation of the college."

added immense tracts which by the time of his death amounted to one hundred and eighty thousand acres of the best lands in Virginia. The extent of Byrd's personal wealth is not known, because his will has been lost, but it is probable that he owned many slaves and other personal property. The brick mansion at Westover was handsomely furnished with furniture that had been brought from England, and there was a great abundance of fine portraits and expensive silverware.

Through Byrd's influence the towns of Richmond and Petersburg were established. Richmond was laid off in 1733 near the falls of James River on property owned by Byrd. He offered the lots for sale on reasonable terms, provided that houses should be built on them in three-years' time. The city, which received its name from the town of Richmond, not far from London, England, was chartered as a town in 1742. Petersburg was laid off about the same time and named for Peter Jones. These sites were selected because they were at the head of navigation on the James and Appomattox rivers.

Byrd was a delightful and witty writer and his books are still charming reading. From his writings one gets a good account of the social life of the time. In a book which he called, "A Progress to the Mines," he de-

scribed a journey from Westover to Germanna, where
Governor Spotswood lived.   Of his arrival at Germanna
he wrote: "Here I arrived about three o'clock and
found only Mrs. Spotswood at home, who received her
old acquaintance with
many a gracious
smile. I was carried
into a room elegantly
set off with pier
glasses the largest of
which came soon
after to an odd mis-
fortune.   Amongst
other strange ani-
mals that cheered
this lady's solitude, a
brace of tame deer
ran familiarly about

THE COAT OF ARMS OF COLONEL BYRD.

the house, and one of them came to stare at me as a
stranger.   But unluckily spying his own figure in the
glass, he made a spring over the tea table that stood
under it and shattered the glass to pieces, and falling
back upon the tea table made a terrible fracas among
the china."

After remaining with Governor Spotswood for a week,
during which time he visited the iron works of the

governor, Byrd began his homeward trip and toward evening arrived at Fredericksburg, of which town the only inhabitants were Colonel Willis, a merchant, a tailor, a smith and an inn-keeper. Byrd spent the night with Colonel Willis, and the next day he proceeded to Major Ben Robinson's. "The major received us with his usual good humor. He has a very industrious wife who has kept him from sinking by the weight of gaming and idleness, but he is now reformed from these ruinous qualities, and by the help of a clerk's place in a quarrelsome county (Caroline) will soon be able to clear his old scores. We drank exceedingly good cider here, the juice of the white apple, which made us talkative until ten o'clock, and then I was conducted to a bed-chamber in which there was neither chair nor table." The next morning he had toast and cider for breakfast and started on his journey. "In about ten miles," Byrd reached Caroline Courthouse where Colonel Armistead and Colonel Beverly had "each of them erected an ordinary well supplied with wine and other polite liquors for the worshipful bench. Such liberal supplies of strong drink often make Justice nod and drop the scales out of her hands."

Two days later Byrd reached his plantation in King William county, where he found his overseers hard at work. For one night he stopped at the home of Mrs. Sym,

10

a portly widow, who at first thought the colonel was a
lover. She was "a person of a lively and cheerful disposition, with much less reserve than most of her
country women. It becomes her very well, and sets
off her other agreeable qualities to advantage." For
supper she gave Byrd "a bottle of honest port" and a
broiled chicken.

From here he went to another plantation where Richmond now stands. Byrd was something of a doctor
and fearing that some of his people at this plantation
might become sick, he left the following prescription:
"To let them blood immediately about eight ounces;
the next day to give them a dose of Indian physic
and to repeat the dose the day following, unless the
symptoms have abated. In the meantime they should
eat nothing but chicken broth and poached eggs and
drink nothing but a quarter of a pint of milk boiled with
a quart of water, and medicated with a little mullen
root or that of the pricky pear."

In his "History of the Dividing Line,"* Byrd has
given some very interesting accounts of North Carolina.
He said: "Surely there is no place in the world where
the inhabitants live with less labor than in North Carolina. The men for their parts, just like the Indians,
impose all the work on the poor women. They make

* For Byrd's Works see Bassett's "Writings of Col. William Byrd."

their wives rise out of their beds early in the morning, at the same time that they lie and snore until the sun has run one-third of his course. Then, after stretching and yawning half an hour, they light their pipes and venture out into the open air, though if it happens to be ever so little cold, they quickly return shivering to the chimney corner. When the weather is mild, they stand leaning with both their arms upon the cornfield fence and gravely consider whether they had best go and take a small heat at the hoe, but generally find reasons to put it off until another time. Most of the rum they get in this country comes from New England and is so bad and unwholesome, that it is not improperly called "Kill devil." It is distilled there from foreign molasses. Their molasses comes from the same country (New England) and has the name of "long sugar" in North Carolina, I suppose from the ropiness of it, and serves all the purposes of sugar both in their eating and drinking." Byrd has told many other interesting things which you should know. The extracts quoted from his books will give you some idea, however, of the way in which he wrote, and at the same time some information about the life of the times. Much of Byrd's time was spent in collecting books, and he also wrote many interesting letters to his prominent friends in England.

William Byrd died in 1744 and was buried in the garden at Westover. He was a splendid representative of the old Virginian, being a man of fine education and scholarly attainments, with a deep interest in

THE TOMB OF WILLIAM BYRD.

the politics and development of his colony. At Westover, he lived like an English lord, and entertained the planters from all parts of Virginia. His home was known for its hospitality, elegance and good company.

Review Questions.

Give an account of colonial plantations and homes. How did the people dress? What were their amusements? Who was "King Carter?" Give an account of William Byrd's life. Tell of his property. What books did he write? Tell of his trip to Germanna, and his return. What does he say about the North Carolinans? What offices did he hold? What kind of a man was Byrd?

Geography Study.

Map of Virginia.—Find Rappahannock, Potomac, James and Appomattox rivers, Charles City county, Spottsylvania county, Caroline county, King William county, Richmond, Petersburg and Fredericksburg.

CHAPTER XII.

ANDREW LEWIS.

1716(?)-1781.

A SHORT while after Joyst Hite settled near where Winchester now stands, then a part of Spotsylvania county, John Lewis came with his family into the upper Valley, and settled in the present Augusta county.

Lewis was an Irishman, of the rank of a gentleman, and his wife, Margaret Lynn, was of noble ancestry. In Ireland, he lived on the property of a cruel lord, who, becoming jealous of the prosperity of his tenant, tried to make Lewis give up his lease. When the latter refused, the nobleman came with some men, attacked Lewis's house, and firing upon it without notice, killed an invalid brother. This so enraged Lewis that, with his servants, he killed the nobleman and his steward. He thereupon fled from Ireland, came to America, and was the first white man to settle in Augusta county. His home was only a few miles from Staunton, which city he founded.

Soon after Lewis had settled in the Valley, he visited

Williamsburg, where he met with Benjamin Borden, who, greatly pleased with Lewis's accounts of the Valley, decided to cross the Blue Ridge and to explore that region. At that time buffaloes roamed in the Valley, and one day the sons of John Lewis caught a little

A SETTLER'S HUT IN THE SHENANDOAH VALLEY.

buffalo calf which they presented to Borden. On returning to Williamsburg, Borden gave it to Governor Gooch, who was so delighted with this unusual pet that he authorized Borden to take up five hundred thousand acres of land at the headwaters of the Shenandoah and James rivers (Augusta and Rockbridge counties), on the condition that he would send settlers into the Valley.

Borden at once brought colonists from England, and soon there were thriving settlements in this region, then a part of Orange county. In 1738 the country west of the Blue Ridge was organized into two counties: one called Frederick, and the other Augusta.*

The early inhabitants of the Valley were chiefly Irish Presbyterians, who, being of Scotch extraction, were called Scotch-Irish. Though everybody in Virginia was supposed to conform to the Church of England, yet in order that settlements might be encouraged in the western part of Virginia, Governor Gooch allowed these Presbyterians to build homes in the Valley without molestation. They made a splendid defence for the frontier, and as a people were "firm, enterprising, hardy and brave." Being violently opposed to any form of tyranny, they were among the first to take an active part against the king at the time of the Revolution.

The Lewises were Scotch-Irish, and their lives clearly indicate what type of men they were. The eldest son of John Lewis was Thomas, who, on account of his poor eyesight, could not take part in the Indian wars which harassed the settlers on the frontier. He was, however, a man of prominence in Augusta, which county he rep-

* Augusta then included all the territory now embraced in southwest Virginia and the seven states of West Virginia, Kentucky, Ohio, Indiana, Illinois, Michigan and Wisconsin, though as yet no pioneers had crossed the Alleghanies.

resented in the House of Burgesses, when he voted in favor of Patrick Henry's famous resolutions of 1765 opposing the Stamp Act. He was a member of the Constitutional Convention that formed the first Virginia constitution and of the convention which ratified the constitution of the United States in 1788. His home was in that part of Augusta which was made into Rockingham county in 1778.

Another son of John was William, who fought in many wars against the Indians, and was an officer in the Revolutionary army, when Tarleton drove the Virginia legislature from Charlottesville. At that time William Lewis was unable to go to the defence of his state on account of sickness, but his wife told her three sons, who were only thirteen, fifteen and seventeen years of age, to prepare for war, saying: "Go, my children, keep back the foot of the invader from the soil of Augusta or see my face no more." When this story was reported to Washington, he said, "Leave me but a banner to plant upon the mountains of Augusta, and I will rally around me the men who will lift our bleeding country from he dust and set her free."

For daring deeds, Charles Lewis, the youngest son, was well known, and many a story has been repeated about him around the firesides of the Valley. On one occasion Charles was taken prisoner by the Indians, who, having bound his hands behind him, were marching him barefooted across the Alleghanies. All the while he was looking for an opportunity to escape. Finally, as he was passing along the edge of a deep ravine through which ran a swift mountain stream, he plunged fearlessly over the precipice, and as he did so, he succeeded in breaking the cords which bound his hands. The Indians jumped after, and chased him down the ravine. But he ran across a field, leaped over some fallen trees, and hid himself in the tall weeds. The Indians failed to find him, although they made a long and faithful search. While Lewis was lying hid in the grass, he perceived a huge rattlesnake coiled and ready to attack him. He knew that if he shuddered or winked his eye even, that the rattlesnake would strike, so he kept perfectly still for more than an hour, until the rattlesnake crossed over his body and crawled away. Charles Lewis became a major in the Virginia militia, and fell bravely fighting the Indians at Point Pleasant.

But the best known of the sons of John Lewis was General Andrew Lewis, who was born in Ireland, probably about the year 1716. In personal appearance he was very imposing, being more than six feet high. He had a giant's frame and the "earth seemed to rumble under him as he walked along." He was stern of countenance, and repulsive to those who did not know him well. To the Indians, the mention of his name brought terror.

When a very young man he was engaged in many fights with the Indians, for hardly had the Valley been settled, before Indians from the borders of the Ohio River crossed the Alleghanies, destroyed many homes and killed many settlers. Among the first to take arms against the savages were the Lewis brothers.

In 1756, Governor Dinwiddie determined to send an expedition against the Shawnee Indians, who lived on the Ohio River near the mouth of Big Sandy River. For this undertaking, Major Andrew Lewis was selected to command the forces. His little army had a long march through a great wilderness, for there were few settlements west of the Alleghany Mountains,

STATUE OF LEWIS.

the first settlers having gone to that region about 1748. After a month's time all of the provisions of the little army had been consumed, but the troops managed to live upon the elks and buffaloes that they shot in the forests. Lewis, failing to find the Indians, returned to Augusta. Governor Dinwiddie was displeased because nothing had been accomplished, and wrote that "Major Lewis and his men did not know the way to the Shawnese towns." Although Lewis had been unsuccessful in this expedition, the governor soon afterwards sent him with a force into the Cherokee country. Hither Lewis proceeded and built a fort on the Tennessee River about thirty miles south of the present site of Knoxville.

In the meantime it was reported that the French and Indians were marching from Fort Duquesne (Pittsburg, Pa.), and were going to attack Winchester, so the governor called out the militia of ten counties to serve under Washington. Lewis was ordered to raise a company of Cherokees and to join Washington, but the Indians were unwilling to serve, and when Lewis returned from the Cherokee country, he brought only seven warriors and three women instead of four hundred warriors as had been expected. Governor Dinwiddie was again greatly disappointed, but he then learned that the Virginians could not hope to enlist the Southern Indians to fight the French and the Indians of the Northwest.

The people of Augusta were in constant fear of the Indian raids, so long as the French remained in control of the Northwest; therefore, Lewis kept the militia of the county in readiness for any emergency. Great was their joy when it became known that William Pitt,

the great English statesman, was determined to capture
Fort Duquesne and Quebec, and drive the French from
North America. General Forbes was sent (1758) to
take Fort Duquesne, and Washington joined him with
about eighteen hundred Virginia soldiers, of whom two
companies were under the command of Major Andrew
Lewis.

On arriving in the neighborhood of Fort Duquesne,
Forbes sent Major Grant with eight hundred men, including Major Lewis
and his two com-
panies, to recon-
noiter the place.
Grant, refusing to

AN INDIAN TOMAHAWK.

take advice, allowed himself to be entrapped by the
Indians. Lewis was left to guard the baggage, while
Grant and his troops went to examine the condition
of the garrison. Suddenly Grant was attacked by
the Indians, who, hidden behind trees, could not be
seen, and the British regulars were driven back with
great loss. Lewis, hearing the noise of the battle,
hastened with his troops to the scene of action.
He and his men were attacked by the Indians with
tomahawk and scalping-knife. Lewis fought hand to
hand with an Indian warrior whom he killed. Finding
himself surrounded by the Indians, he surrendered to

a French soldier in order to save his life. He was treated with great indignity, stripped of all his clothing and carried a prisoner to the fort. It is not known how long he remained in prison, but he was probably released when General Forbes captured Fort Duquesne. After the French were driven out of the Northwest, there were few Indian raids into Augusta county, and for some time we hear little of Lewis.

Settlers came in great numbers to the Valley, so that by 1769 it was felt that Augusta county ought to be again divided. The southern part, then including all of southwest Virginia, was cut off and made into the County of Botetourt. In this section, not far from the present site of Salem, Andrew Lewis lived, and when Botetourt was formed, he was made a justice of the peace for that county. ▪

In 1774 the governor of Virginia was Lord Dunmore. Many settlers had by this time pushed their way across the Alleghany Mountains, and some had their eyes turned to Kentucky; but as yet no county had been organized west of the Alleghanies. The Indians along the Ohio River, fearing that they would lose their lands, rose against the whites, burned many settlements and killed the settlers. In retaliation some of the frontiersmen had attacked and killed the entire family of an Indian chief, named Logan. This brought on a general war along the frontier, and Lord Dunmore at once prepared to defend the western settlements.

Andrew Lewis was appointed brigadier general, and forthwith he raised a force of eleven hundred men chiefly from Augusta, Botetourt, Culpeper and Bedford counties. These men were bold and brave frontiersmen. "They wore fringed hunting shirts dyed yellow, white, brown and even red. Quaintly carved shot-bags and powder-horns hung from their broad belts. They had fur caps, or soft hats, moccasins and coarse woolen leggins reaching half

LORD DUMMORE.

way up to the thigh. Each carried his flint-lock, his tomahawk and scalping knife."

With such men Lewis marched from Lewisburg, in what is now Greenbrier county, one hundred and sixty miles through the wilderness to the juncture of the Ohio and the Kanawha rivers, and took up his position on the point of land between the rivers, known as Point Pleasant. Here he expected to be joined by Lord Dunmore, who commanded an army raised in Frederick and the adjoining counties in northern Virginia. Dunmore did not arrive, but sent messages to Lewis that he had gone to attack the Shawnese towns across the Ohio, and ordered Lewis to cross the river and join him. Before Lewis could obey, he was attacked by the Indian leader, Cornstalk, with two thousand men. The battle was a fierce and bloody struggle, and was a sort of single combat. The fighting was done at close range. Each man sheltered himself behind a stump, a rock or a tree trunk. The Indians fully expected to gain the victory, but the frontiersmen under Andrew Lewis were too valiant for their enemy. When the savages began to waver, the voice of Cornstalk could be heard above the din of battle calling to his warriors: "Be strong! Be strong!" After a desperate resistance, the Indians broke and fled. The victory was decisive, but an expensive one. "The loss of the Virginians was heavy. Two colonels, seven captains, three lieutenants, and seventy-five men were killed, and one hundred and forty wounded. Out of every five men one was dead or wounded." The Indians lost even more heavily, and were never again able to meet the Virginians in open battle.*

* We are not to suppose, however, that there were not Indian raids from time to time. These occurred frequently, and every pioneer barred his doors at night and kept his gun at the head of his bed as he slept, not knowing at what time the Indians might attack. The women, as well as the men, often engaged in warfare against the Indians. Such a woman was "Mad Ann" of Alleghany county, the wife of John Bailey, a soldier killed at the battle of Point Pleasant.

In less than a year after the battle of Point Pleasant, the Revolutionary war was at hand, and the Virginians were preparing to drive Lord Dunmore from the colony. It was believed that Dunmore had encouraged the Indians at Point Pleasant, so that the Virginians might be made too weak to contend with England. Whether this be true or not, Lord Dunmore was certainly an unprincipled man. The honor of having driven him out of Virginia belongs to Andrew Lewis. When the Revolutionary war opened, at Washington's request, Andrew Lewis accepted a brigadier-generalship in the army, and early in 1776 he took charge of the Virginia troops stationed at Williamsburg.*

Before this time Lord Dunmore, for fear of the Virginia people, had left Williamsburg on his warship *Fowey*,

She went about dressed in a woman's skirt and a man's coat, a rifle on her shoulder and a tomahawk and butcher knife in her belt. She could climb the steepest mountain whether it was severe winter or hot summer. She often left home and no one knew her whereabouts, and when she returned, she always brought the scalps of some Indians. Sometimes she engaged in hand to hand fights with the Indians. She lived to be a very old woman and died in 1825, almost within the memory of our fathers. Her story is but an indication of the rough pioneer life before and after the time of the Revolution. With the battle of Point Pleasant, open warfare with the Indians was at an end, but the settlers, like "Mad Ann," often had to hunt their enemy as they would hunt wolves.

*The story is told that Washington wanted Lewis to be made commander-in-chief, but Congress forced the position on himself. He recommended Lewis for a major-generalship, but Congress set him aside in the interest of one of its favorites.

and had seized Norfolk. Colonel Woodford of Caroline county was sent against him, and at Great Bridge, about twelve miles from Norfolk, a detachment of the British had been defeated, whereupon Lord Dunmore had been forced to abandon Norfolk. In May, 1776, Lord Dunmore with five hundred men including the negro slaves whom he had stolen from the Virginians, had established himself at Gwyn's Island in the Chesapeake Bay on the east side of Matthews county. Lewis at once went to Matthews county to drive Dunmore away, or to capture him. Two batteries having been planted on the shores, a vigorous cannonade was opened against Dunmore's fleet which lay between the shore and the island. The fleet was badly damaged. The next day Lewis sent Colonel McClanahan with two hundred men to the island, but before he could land, the English had made their escape. When Dunmore sailed from Gwyn's Island, he left Virginia never to return.

What loss Lewis inflicted on Dunmore's troops is not known. One hundred and thirty graves were counted on the island and many dead bodies were found, but most of the deaths were due to the smallpox which had raged on the fleet and among the slaves whom he had taken from their masters.

For four years of the Revolutionary war, Lewis served

as a brigadier general, in which position he never had a good opportunity to display his military genuis. In 1780 he resigned his command in the army, probably on account of ill health. He started home, but on reaching Colonel Buford's in Bedford county, he was taken ill and died. His body was carried across the Blue Ridge and buried on his plantation, "Dropmore," near Salem,

LEWIS'S GRAVE AT SALEM.

in what is now Roanoke county, but at that time a part of Botetourt.

Lewis's services to Virginia should never be forgotten. He, above all others, saved Virginia from the Indians, and drove from the state Lord Dunmore, the most unworthy governor that Virginia ever had. In 1857, when the famous Washington monument in the capitol square at Richmond was unveiled, Virginia did honor to the services of Lewis by placing his statue (see page 155) on that monument along with Mason, Jefferson, Marshall, Henry and Nelson.   There you may see Lewis in the dress of a western pioneer, with his trusty hunting knife at his side and his faithful rifle in his hand.

Review Questions.

Give some account of John Lewis. What position did Thomas Lewis hold? Tell about William Lewis and his sons. Tell the story of Charles Lewis's escape from the Indians. Tell what kind of looking man Andrew Lewis was. Tell of his trip to find the Shawnee Indians. Give an account of his trip to the Cherokee country. Tell of his capture by the French and Indians. Describe the battle of Point Pleasant. Tell the story of "Mad Ann." Tell of Dunmore's defeat at Great Bridge. How did Lewis drive Dunmore from Virginia? Tell of Lewis's death and burial. How has Virginia honored him?

Geography Study.

Map of Virginia.—Find Spotsylvania, Orange, Augusta, Alleghany, Frederick, Botetourt, Roanoke, Washington, Culpeper, Matthews, Rockingham, Bedford and Rockbridge counties; Salem, Winchester, Williamsburg, Norfolk and Gwyn's Island. *Map of West Virginia.*—Find Greenbrier county, Lewisburg, Ohio River, Kanawha River and Point Pleasant.

CHAPTER XIII.

PATRICK HENRY.

1736-1799.

WHILE Virginia was increasing in population, and settlements were being formed west of the Blue Ridge, the English government was looking with jealousy upon the prosperity of her colonies in America. In the year 1765 the English Parliament determined to impose a tax upon the American people, and it thereupon passed a law known as the Stamp Act.

By this measure the colonies were required to use stamps, made and furnished by the English government, upon all newspapers and books published in America, and upon documents of all kinds (wills, deeds, etc.), in order that they might be legal. The colonies north and south regarded this action of the English government as tyranny, claiming that they should not be taxed since they had no representation in the English Parliament. Virginia was the first colony to enter a formal protest, and the leader in the bold step was Patrick Henry, the prophet and orator of the Revolution.

Henry was a native of Hanover county. His father and his uncle, both men of learning, taught Henry the rudiments of Latin, Greek and mathematics.   But since Patrick was not a book - loving boy, at an early age he began work by keeping store. Failing at this business, he made a venture of another kind, and though only nineteen years old, he married Sarah Shelton, the daughter of a small farmer of the neighborhood. His father and father-in-law came to his aid and placed him on a small farm with two slaves.   He was un-

PATRICK HENRY.

successful at farming, and again tried storekeeping with no better results.

Henry was a great lover of music and dancing. He read little, but learned much from those with whom he came in contact. He was fond of talking, and could tell a joke with wonderful effect. These were qualities which Henry thought would make a lawyer; he therefore secured an old English law book and a copy of the Virginia laws, which he studied for only six weeks. He then went to Williamsburg and took an examination before the judges of Virginia, who easily discovered that Henry had little knowledge of law, but seeing that he was a man of good common sense, they finally granted him his license to practice (1760).

In 1763 the famous Parson's Case came up in Hanover county. As you have learned, the law of Virginia fixed the salary of a preacher at sixteen thousand pounds of tobacco ($640). At that time tobacco was worth two pennies a pound, but it gradually increased in price until it came to be worth six pennies a pound. Thereupon, the House of Burgesses passed a law saying that the ministers should be paid in money at the rate of two pennies a pound for tobacco; in other words, preachers were to receive as much pay as had been given them before tobacco increased in value. This act could not become a binding law in Virginia until it met with the approval of the king, but on being sent to England he rejected it. In the meantime, the Virginians had gone on as if the law was binding and had paid the preachers in money. Since the king had not approved of the Virginia law, the clergy demanded their sixteen thousand pounds of tobacco, or its then market value ($2,000).

As a test case, Mr. Maury, a minister of Hanover county, brought suit to secure the difference between what had been received in money and the value of the tobacco. As the champion of the people, Patrick Henry appeared in the case when it was called at Hanover Courthouse. That was a great day in Henry's life, for from that time he was expected to lead in all movements for liberty. On the day of the trial about twenty ministers were present, and out of respect they were invited to sit by the magistrates who were then the judges in Virginia. One of the preachers was Henry's uncle, and his father was one of the magistrates. When Henry rose to address the jury he was so awkward in appearance and halting in speech, that the people felt that their cause was lost. But soon the young man rose on tiptoe, and in fiery eloquence argued for the rights of the people against the king and the established church. So severe was his denunciation of the king that several persons shouted, "Treason! Treason!", but to no avail; for the young orator believed that he was pleading a righteous cause. He made such an impression on the jury, that in less than five minutes they brought in a verdict of one penny damages for the Rev. Mr. Maury.

Two years later Henry was a member of the House of Burgesses from Louisa county. When the assembly met at Williamsburg, every member was discussing the recent Stamp Act which had been passed by the Eng-

THE COURTHOUSE AT HANOVER, VIRGINIA.

lish Parliament. Henry's very blood boiled that England should try to tax the colonies without their consent, and he doubtless remembered the attack which he had made on the king in his speech at Hanover Courthouse in the Parson's Case. He thereupon wrote five resolutions in which he boldly asserted that the right to govern Virginia lay in the House of Burgesses and not in the English Parliament. When these resolutions were offered, many of the members, especially those from eastern Virginia, opposed them bitterly. Henry at once rose to his feet, and made a memorable speech, of which the closing words were: "Caesar had his Brutus; Charles I. his Cromwell; and George III. . . ." Many of the members rose to their feet at this point and cried, "Treason, Treason," but Henry only paused and said: "George III. may profit by their example. If this be treason, make the most of it." The resolutions were passed by a majority of only one vote. Among those who voted against them were some of the most prominent men of the colony, such as Peyton Randolph, Edmund Pendleton and George Wythe. Jefferson, then a law student in Williamsburg, heard Randolph say as he came out of the house, "I would have given five hundred guineas for a vote."

On the afternoon of that day (29th of May), Patrick Henry returned home. He passed up the Duke of Gloucester Street "wearing buckskin breeches, his saddle bags on his arm, leading a lean horse and chatting with Paul Carrington (a burgess from Charlotte county), who walked by his side."

The next day the House of Burgesses seemed to fear what it had done and repealed the fifth section of Henry's resolution which declared "that the General Assembly of this colony have the sole exclusive right and power to levy taxes." The conservative Burgesses were not yet ready for so bold a protest. Unlike Henry, they had not seen that war was to come and that the colonies would eventually declare themselves independent. Henry's resolutions were the first blow of the Revolution.

The English Parliament soon after repealed the Stamp Act, but refused to give up the right to tax the

ST. JOHN'S CHURCH AT RICHMOND, VIRGINIA

colonies and passed a law to tax tea, paper and some other articles which might be brought to America. The Virginians did not quietly submit, but claimed that they should not be taxed without representation in the English Parliament. On finding out that England insisted on taxing the colonies, the House of Burgesses passed, in 1769, another series of .resolutions which were much like those that Henry had introduced in 1765.

In 1773 a committee of correspondence was appointed

in Virginia to keep in touch with the other English colonies. Peyton Randolph was chairman of this committee, and the other members were Pendleton, Henry, Jefferson, Bland, Richard Henry Lee, Archibald Cary, Dabney Carr, Dudley, Diggs, Benjamin Harrison and Robert C. Nicholas.

While this controversy was going on between England and her colonies, Henry was growing in reputation as lawyer and a leader. He had been admitted to practice before the General Court of Virginia. His resolutions of 1765 had made him · known throughout the colonies. When the first Continental Congress met in Philadelphia (1774), the Virginia representatives were Peyton Randolph, Richard Henry Lee, George Washington, Patrick Henry, Richard Bland, Benjamin Harrison and Edmund Pendleton. Peyton Randolph was elected president of this body.

Henry urged that the colonies should act together, and said: "The distinctions between the Virginians, Pennsylvanians, New Yorkers and New Englanders are no more. I am not a Virginian, but an American." Without a doubt, Henry and Richard Henry Lee were the leading debaters and orators of the first Continental Congress. The Congress appealed to the English government to redress their grievances, and to the people of the colonies to stand firmly by their rights.

Henry was a member of the Virginia conventions of 1774 and 1775. The convention of 1775 met in March at old St. John's Church in Richmond. At the very opening of the convention Henry moved that the colony of Virginia should at once raise troops to defend itself against England. His resolutions were opposed by some members on the ground that there was no war with England. Henry spoke in defence of his resolutions and closed his speech by saying: "Our brethern are already in the field. Why stand we here idle? What is it that the gentlemen wish? What would they have? Is life so dear, or peace so sweet, as to be purchased at the price of chains and slavery? Forbid it, Almighty God; I know not what course others may take, but, as for me, give me liberty or give me death." His speech carried all before him. The resolutions were passed, troops were at once raised, and Henry was made commander-in-chief of the Virginia forces.

He, indeed, spoke as a prophet when he said: "The next gale that sweeps from the north will bring to our ears the clash of resounding arms." Hardly had Virginia begun to raise troops before the news came that the first battle of the Revolution had been fought at Lexington and Concord in Massachusetts.

In April of this same year, Lord Dunmore removed secretly from the old Powder Horn at Williamsburg all the ammunition that was kept there. When Henry heard of this action, he at once advanced with the Virginia troops towards Williamsburg. The people of the colony rose on all sides to join him, and we are told that

THE OLD POWDER HORN AT WILLIAMSBURG.

he had with him more than five thousand men. Lord Dunmore became alarmed and sent messengers to Henry asking him to disband his troops, but he continued his march until he was within sixteen miles of Williamsburg. The governor's family fled from the capital and war would probably have broken out at that time, had not

Lord Dunmore paid more than a thousand dollars for the powder which he had removed. A few months later Dunmore left Williamsburg never to return again.

The colony being without a head, the Convention of 1776 drew up a constitution and elected Patrick Henry as the first governor. For three years he held this responsible position and showed that he was a man of power and ability. In 1784 he was again called to the governor's chair and served for two years.

When Virginia's convention met in 1788 to pass upon the Constitution of the United States, Henry was a member of that body. He did all in his power to prevent the adoption of the Constitution, because he saw that the day would come when some of the states would regret that they had ever entered the Union.

The people of Virginia idolized Henry, and they would have given him any office in their power. He never sought office, but the office sought him. He declined to be a member of the Federal Convention of 1787. He could have been United States Senator, the Secretary of State under Washington, or Chief Justice of the United States, but he declined all these honors. In 1796 he was a third time elected governor of Virginia, but at once refused to accept the position. Three years later, when he thought that the affairs of our country were in a serious condition, he stood for the legislature in Charlotte county and was elected, but before he could take his seat, he died.

In the latter part of his life Henry had fallen into debt and he went back to the practice of law to regain his for-

From an old print.

RED HILL, THE HOME OF PATRICK HENRY.

tune.   He was counsel for Thomas Walker in the British Debts case, in which an Englishman brought suit against Mr. Walker for a debt made before the Revolution.   It is said that for weeks before the trial Henry shut himself up from all other engagements to study the case.   When it was argued before the Federal Court at Richmond, he thrilled the whole room with his eloquence.

Another case in which Henry figured was against one John Hook, a Scotchman, who brought suit for some beeves which had been taken from his plantation by the

American soldiers during the Revolutionary War. Mr. Henry made a strong appeal, showing that a man of patriotism would never have demanded pay. He carried his hearers in imagination to Yorktown and the surrender of Cornwallis. He pictured Washington standing amid the joy of the occasion, when a note of discord was heard, and behold it was John Hook hoarsely bawling through the American camp, "Beef, Beef, Beef." The people were convulsed with laughter. The case was submitted to the jury and at once a verdict was rendered against Hook. So intense was public feeling against him that some of the people at quiet old Campbell Courthouse raised the cry of "tar and feathers," and Hook saved himself by mounting his horse and riding swiftly away.

Patrick Henry had many homes,* but four years before his death, he took up his residence at the beautiful estate of "Red Hill," in Charlotte county. Here, having paid his debts and given up the practice of law, he spent the rest of his life. Every morning when the

* He first lived in Hanover county, where he bought a plantation known as "Scotchdown." While he was governor of the commonwealth, he resided at Williamsburg, but when the capitol was removed to Richmond, he located in that city. For a time he lived at "Salisbury" in Chesterfield county. He afterwards bought a home with ten thousand acres of land known as "Leatherwood" in Henry county, which was named for him. Later he lived on the Appomattox River in Prince Edward county, and then at "Long Island" in Campbell county.

12

weather was warm and pleasant, he was accustomed to sit with his chair leaning against one of the trees on the lawn around his house.   He delighted in his family, and often a visitor would find him lying on the floor romping with the children, or playing the fiddle for them to dance. He used no wine or alcoholic stimulants and detested tobacco.   He was a person of strong religious faith. For love of country and nobility of character, he is to be ranked among the great Virginians.

Review Questions.

What was the Stamp Act ?   Tell of Henry's early life and his admission to the bar.   Explain the Parson's case.   Why did Henry win in that case ?   Give an account of the resolutions of 1765.   What did Peyton Randolph say ?   How did Henry look as he went out of Williamsburg?   What were the resolutions of 1769?   What was the committee of correspondence of 1773?   Tell of Henry in the Continental Congress of 1774.   Give an account of his speech before the Virginia convention of 1775.   Tell how he made Dunmore pay for the powder.   How many years was he governor ?   What offices did he decline ?   Why did he oppose the adoption of the Constitution of the United States ?   Tell of his homes and of his last years.

Geography Study.

Map of Virginia.—Find Hanover, Chesterfield, Campbell, Henry, Charlotte, Louisa, and Prince Edward counties, and locate their courthouses.   Find Richmond and Williamsburg. *Map of Pennsylvania.*—Locate Philadelphia.   How would you go from Williamsburg to Philadelphia ?

CHAPTER XIV.

GEORGE WASHINGTON.

1732–1799.

WESTMORELAND county gave to Virginia and our country George Washington, "the noblest figure that ever stood in the forefront of a nation's life." Washington was born on the 22d day of February, 1732. His birthplace was on Bridges Creek not far from the Potomac River. The house contained four rooms on the ground floor, an attic with a sloping roof and a large brick chimney. Three years after his birth the family removed to Stafford county, just across

THE MOTHER OF GEORGE WASHINGTON.

the river from Fredericksburg. Here his father, Augustine Washington, died when Washington was only eleven years old and he was left to the care of his mother, whose

maiden name was Mary Ball. She was a woman of strong
will, religious and stern, but kind. She was devoted to
George, and as he grew to be a man, she was accustomed to say, "George has been a good boy, and he will
surely do his duty." She taught her son the principles
of truth and honor.

Washington had poor school advantages, but while
in Stafford he was taught reading and writing by the
sexton of the parish, a man named Hobby. Later he
was sent to live with his half-brother, Augustine Washington, in Westmoreland county, in order that he might
receive instruction from a Mr. Williams, who conducted
a fairly good school. Here Washington learned some
mathematics and land surveying. Among the boys,
Washington was leader both in his studies and upon the
play ground. He used to divide his companions into
armies, one of which he always commanded himself.
He excelled his playmates in running, jumping and
wrestling:

The two older brothers, Lawrence and Augustine
Washington, had been educated in England, where many
Virginia boys were sent to school, but on account of the
death of his father, George was deprived of this privi-
lege. In 1747, when he was not quite sixteen, he left
school and went to visit his brother Lawrence, who resided at Mount Vernon, near Alexandria. Here he met

Lord Fairfax, an old bachelor who had come to Virginia to take possession of his large grant of land across the Blue Ridge Mountains. It was the purpose of Lord Fairfax to send settlers into that region, but, before doing so, it was necessary that the country should be surveyed. For this work he found young Washington in every way capable.

Though so young, Washington was robust, nearly six feet tall and well-formed, with long arms and big hands and feet. He had light brown hair and grayish blue eyes, and was a splendid type of a manly boy. In character, too, he was to be admired, for he was honor-

THE ENGLISH COLONIAL TERRITORY IN 1750.

able, persevering in whatever he undertook and wise far beyond his years.

In 1748, accompanied by George Fairfax, a kinsman of Lord Fairfax, Washington crossed over the Blue Ridge into what is now Frederick county, Virginia,

where he began his work.   For three years he remained
as a surveyor.   During this time he suffered many hardships.   He often slept for weeks at a time on the ground
before the camp fire, and often for days at a time his
clothes were wet.   For his work Washington received a
doubloon a day (about eight dollars in our money).   Lord
Fairfax was so pleased with the account of the Shenandoah Valley, that he moved across the Blue Ridge and
built a home there, which he called Greenway Court.
Here Washington was frequently a visitor, and whenever he had a chance, he would read in the library of
Lord Fairfax.   On the recommendation of his lordship, Washington was appointed by the president of
William and Mary College a surveyor of Culpeper county,
which then extended across the mountains.   He was kept
constantly at work, for at this time many Germans
were coming into the northern valley, and a surveyor
was needed to cut off for each man his tract of land.

In 1751 came a sudden change in Washington's career.   Lawrence Washington was taken ill and George
went to nurse him.   A year later Lawrence died, leaving
George as guardian of his little daughter and heir to the
property in the event of her death.   Shortly after this
she died, and the splendid estate of Mount Vernon became the property of George Washington.   At the time
of his brother's death, though only twenty years old,

Washington was appointed major in the Virginia militia, and a year later, when Virginia was divided into four military districts, young Washington was put in command of the northern division.

About this time the French occupied the territory along the upper Ohio River. The Virginians likewise claimed the western lands, and the Ohio company had received a charter for more than five hundred thousand acres of land along the river. The Washington brothers were interested in this company, and Lawrence Washington,

GEORGE WASHINGTON AS A YOUNG MAN.

(*From a painting in possession of General George Washington Custis Lee, of Lexington, Va.*)

just before his death, had been made manager of it. Governor Dinwiddie at once saw that the Virginia claim to the western land was about to be lost by French occupation. He thereupon determined to send an embassy requesting the French to withdraw from the Ohio River, and in the event of their refusal, to send an armed force to establish the English title. He selected as this messenger, George Washington, then but twenty-one years of age. When the French fort was reached, Washington was courteously received by the commander, Chevalier de St. Pierre, an elderly man with silver gray hair. To the message which Washington brought from Governor Dinwiddie he replied: "I am here by the orders of my general, and I entreat you, sir, not to doubt one moment but that I am determined to conform myself to them with all of the exactness and resolution that can be expected from the best officer."

Washington returned as quickly as he could to Virginia, but his trip was a perilous one. It was the middle of winter, and he often had to cross the rivers on ice. On one occasion he broke through, and barely escaped drowning. Once an Indian guide tried to shoot him. On reaching Williamsburg, about the middle of January (1754), he informed Governor Dinwiddie that the French were determined to hold their position. Virginia prepared for war, and appointed Colonel Fry to command the forces with Washington as his lieutenant-colonel. The troops were slow in assembling, so without Colonel Fry, Washington set out from Alexandria with only two companies of soldiers.

When he reached Great Meadows, near the Monongahela River, he had an encounter with the French, whose commander, Jumonville, was killed. Here Washington built a rude fortification which was called Fort Necessity, and in this he placed his three hundred and fifty

Virginians.   The French and Indians made a vigorous
attack and were repulsed, but when Washington perceived the numbers and realized that ammunition was
failing, he decided to surrender the fort, with the provision that his troops, carrying their arms, might quietly
return home.   This was a bitter disappointment, but
Washington did well to get away on these terms, and
the Virginia House of Burgesses, recognizing this fact,
passed a vote of thanks to Washington and his officers.

   The English government now determined to drive the
French from the Ohio Valley, and for that purpose they
sent General Braddock to aid the Virginians.   When he
arrived in Virginia, he talked very boastfully of what he
could do with his regulars, and almost showed contempt
for Washington and the Virginia troops, who were to
help in the campaign.   Braddock proceeded at once
from Alexandria to Fort Duquesne, which the French
had built where Pittsburg (Pa.) now stands.   As
the English were marching recklessly through the dense
wilderness about eight miles from Fort Duquesne they
were suddenly fired upon by the French and Indians who
were hid in the woods.   Though they formed themselves
in their accustomed ranks crying, "God save the King,
God save the King," they were being killed in numbers
when Washington asked Braddock to order his troops
to take to the woods, and fire from behind the trees in

Indian fashion.   It is reported that Braddock was very angry with Washington, replying, "What! a Virginia colonel, teach a British General how to fight!"   The loss of the Virginia and English troops was heavy, and when they broke, it was Washington who gathered up the fugitives and brought from the field Braddock,

WASHINGTON'S HOME AT MOUNT VERNON.

who had received a mortal wound.   Four days later Braddock was buried, and Washington read the solemn words of the English burial services at the grave.

Washington returned to Mount Vernon worn out with his campaign.   He wrote to his mother, "If it is in my power to avoid going to the Ohio again, I shall; but if the command is pressed upon me by the general voice of the country and offered upon such terms as can not be objected against, it would reflect dishonor upon me to refuse it." The very day on which he wrote this letter, the governor offered to him the command of all the Virginia troops on his own terms. Washington accepted and established his headquarters at Winchester,* August, 1755, and had under him Lieutenant-colonel Adam Stephen and Major Andrew Lewis.

Washington's defence of the frontier proved so effective, that soon many settlers came into the Valley, and by 1759 Winchester contained two hundred houses. You have learned in connection with Andrew Lewis that General Forbes undertook an expedition against Fort Duquesne. Washington commanded the Virginia troops and joined General Forbes. It was against Washington's advice that Major Grant with

---

* At this time Winchester was a frontier town, being the only one in the northern valley. There were then but two counties, Frederick and Augusta, west of the Blue Ridge mountains. Virginia had fifty-two counties and forty-four towns, though more than half of the latter had not more than five houses. The population of the colony was about two hundred and ninety-three thousand, of whom one hundred and twenty thousand were negroes.

The Indians, incited by the French, made raids upon the inhabitants of frontier settlements which were beyond the mountains. So in 1756, Major Andrew Lewis, as you have learned, was sent into western Virginia against these Indians, but he did not find them. Major Lewis was also with Washington at Fort Necessity and at Braddock's defeat, and rendered great service.

Major Andrew Lewis was sent to reconnoiter the country about Fort Duquesne. When Forbes moved with the main army against the fort, Washington requested to be put in the front, and Forbes, remembering Braddock's fate, complied with the request. With his sixteen hundred Virginians Washington led the march to Fort Duquesne. In accordance with his advice, also, the army pushed rapidly forward. As a result the French were disconcerted, and abandoned the place. Washington with his Virginians was the first to enter this fort, where he planted with his own hand the English flag (1758). The works were repaired and named Fort Pitt, in honor of the Prime Minister of England. The French were at last driven from the Ohio region.

The people of Frederick elected Washington a member of the House of Burgesses, though he was not a resident of that county. On taking his seat Speaker Robinson thanked him in behalf of the colony for his service in the wars. "Washington rose to express his acknowledgments for the honor, but was so disconcerted as to be unable to articulate a word distinctly. He blushed and faltered for a moment, when the Speaker relieved him from his embarrassment by saying, 'Sit down, Mr. Washington; your modesty equals your valor and that surpasses the power of any language that I possess."

Just before Washington marched with General Forbes

MARTHA WASHINGTON.   GEORGE WASHINGTON.

to Fort Duquesne, he was on his way to Williamsburg to make a report to Governor Dinwiddie. When he was within a few hours' ride of the old capitol he was hailed by Colonel Chamberlayne of New Kent county, who took him to dine at his home. Here Washington met a charming young widow, Mrs. Martha Custis, whom a few months later he led to the altar as his bride. The marriage was performed at St. Peter's Church in New Kent county on January 6, 1759. It was a brilliant company that assembled to witness the wedding of the best soldier in the colony.

Washington now made his home at Mount Vernon, where he enjoyed the free and easy life of a planter. He lived plainly, but sometimes he drove out with his wife and step-children to visit a neighbor or to attend a ball. At times he went fox-hunting with Lord Fairfax, or some of the neighbors. During this period he served in the House of Burgesses.* Washington was a member of the House of Burgesses in 1765 when Patrick Henry took his seat and offered those famous resolutions against the Stamp Act. We do not know how Washington voted, but he probably voted with the Conservatives against Henry's resolutions, though he was opposed to the Stamp Act.

Although England soon repealed the Stamp Act, she still insisted on the right to tax the colonies, and laid duties upon tea and some other articles, which were imported by the colonists. Washington felt that this was an imposition, and he wrote to his friend Mason: "Something should be done to maintain the liberty which we have derived from our ancestors. No man should hesitate a moment to use arms in defense of so valuable a blessing is clearly my opinion. Yet arms, I should beg

* Like other politicians of the day, when election time came on he appeared before the voters and did the usual treating. We are told that when he was first elected a member of the Burgesses, though only a few hundred votes were cast, he paid for his election with a hogshead and a barrel of punch, thirty-five gallons of wine, forty-three gallons of strong cider and dinner for his friends. This cost in money was thirty-nine pounds and six shillings ($200). Jefferson had done the same thing when he was first elected to the Burgesses, and it is said that the people of Orange once failed to elect Madison a member of the legislature because he would not spend money in treating.

leave to suggest, should be the last resource." In 1769, on account of strong resolutions against the English government, the governor dissolved the Burgesses. Thereafter most of them met in the Raleigh Tavern and

THE RALEIGH TAVERN.

adopted some resolutions called the non-importation agreement, drawn by George Mason and presented by Washington, agreeing that none of them would import from England tea or any other taxed goods. Washington lived up to this agreement, and would not allow any tea to be used in his own home.

Shortly after this, by act of English Parliament, the Boston Harbor was closed, and the first Continental Congress met in Philadelphia in 1774. Washington was chosen one of the Virginia representatives to that body, which asked England to repeal her harsh laws against the colonies. Congress adjourned to meet again in May, 1775. Before it reassembled, the first battle of the

Revolution was fought on April 19th, at Concord and Lexington in Massachusetts, and the colonies were in open rebellion against the mother country.

When the second Continental Congress assembled on May 10, 1775, it began immediately to consider what the colonies ought to do, and after a month's time, decided to put an army in the field. Against his wish, Washington was elected as commander-in-chief of the American forces. He proceeded at once to Boston, where he was received with shouts and the firing of cannon. On July 3rd, 1775, he took command of the Continental Army.

The story of the Revolutionary War belongs to the history of the United States, and can not be given here. Sufficient it is to say that from 1775 to 1781, a period of six years, Washington held the English army under check in New York, Pennsylvania and New Jersey. He lost several battles, but never suffered any crushing defeats. By two brilliant victories, one at Trenton and the other at Princeton, he saved the American cause.

His soldiers suffered greatly in the terrible winters, and especially while they were stationed at Valley Forge near Philadelphia, for the winter of 1777–1778. Though the army had scarcely any clothes, shoes or food, Washington did not despair. A less brave man would have succumbed to the neglect of Congress, which had

ample supplies, but did not furnish the means of sending them to the army. A plot was hatched even to
remove Washington from the command, but it failed
to carry, and Washington continued to persevere.
Through the skill of a German officer, Baron Steuben,
the soldiers were kept in constant drill, and when they
were out of winter quarters in the spring, they were
better disciplined than at any time before.

After two years of waiting the time came when the
war should close. Lord Cornwallis with an English
army had stationed himself at Yorktown. A French
fleet had entered the mouth of York River, and thus an
English fleet was prevented from bringing aid. Washington saw the situation and marched rapidly from New
York to Yorktown, where he found Lafayette and the
Virginian troops under Nelson. With Washington was
a strong French force under Count Rochambeau. When
the army was drawn up at Yorktown, it numbered in
all twelve thousand men. Gradually the lines of the
Americans were moved closer and closer, and each day
the English were subjected to a heavy fire. After a
siege of three weeks, Cornwallis decided to surrender,
and on the 19th of October, 1781, the English marched
between the Americans and French drawn up in separate
lines, and laid down their arms, while the band played
"The World Turned Upside Down."

13

The war was now at an end, and in 1783 England acknowledged the independence of the thirteen states. During the long struggle Washington had been unselfishly patriotic. At one time the army was ready to declare him king, but Washington sternly rejected such a proposition.

In December, 1783, he bade farewell to the officers of the army in Fraunces's Tavern, New York. To those men who had followed him through the long and dark contest, he said : "With a heart full of love and gratitude I now take my leave of you, most devoutly wishing that your latter days may be as prosperous and happy as your former ones have been glorious and honorable." In silence and with tears in his eyes he embraced each officer, after which he walked to Whitehall Ferry and began his journey homeward. He went to Annapolis (Md.), where he resigned his commission to Congress, and on Christmas Eve, 1783, reached Mt. Vernon, which he had left eight years before to become commander-in-chief of the Continental army.

In 1787 a convention met in Philadelphia to draw up a constitution for the United States. Washington was one of the Virginia delegates, and was made president of the convention. When the constitution went into effect, in 1789, Washington was elected as the first President of the United States, having received every

FEDERAL HALL, NEW YORK, WHERE WASHINGTON WAS INAUGURATED PRESIDENT.

vote cast. It was with some regret that he left Mt. Vernon to go to New York, where Congress was then in session. His journey was made by carriage, and all along the road he was received with great delight by a loving people. On reaching New York he was conducted to Federal Hall, where, on the 30th of April, 1789, he was inaugurated President amid the shouts of "God bless our Washington! Long live our beloved Washington!"

Washington was elected to a second term and declined a third. For eight years he presided with dignity and success over the affairs of the United States.

On retiring from the Presidency, he returned to Mount Vernon, where he led the life of an unaffected Virginia gentleman. Though he had been President of the United States, he did not refuse to serve on a jury in his native county when asked to do so.

On the 12th of December, 1799, while riding over his farm, he was chilled by the keen winds and by the cold rain and sleet that was falling. When he retired that night, he was hoarse and cold, and in the night he awoke with a sharp pain in his throat. In the morning a doctor was summoned and the usual treatment of bleeding and other remedies were applied, but nothing would relieve the trouble, and he died on December 14, 1799. His body lies buried upon Virginia soil in a simple, but imposing tomb at Mount Vernon. In 1857, the State of Virginia erected to his memory a splendid equestrian statue which adorns the capitol square at Richmond.*

Washington was a gallant soldier and a statesman, and a high-minded gentleman of dauntless courage and stainless honor. Virginia will always be proud that she furnished to the Union him of whom it has been truly said that he was "first in war, first in peace, first in the hearts of his countrymen."

> " He knew not North, nor South, nor West, nor East :
>   Childless himself, Father of States he stood,

*See p. 10.

Strong and sagacious as a Knight turned Priest,
   And avowed to deeds of good.

So his vast image shadows all the lands,
   So holds forever Man's adoring eyes,
And o'er the Union which it left it stands
   Our Cross against the sky !" *

Review Questions.

Tell of the early life of Washington. Give some of his experiences as a surveyor. Give some account of Lord Fairfax. Tell of his brother Lawrence Washington's death and will. Tell of Washington's trip to ask the French to leave the Ohio Region. Give the story of the surrender of Fort Necessity. Give an account of Braddock's defeat. Tell of Winchester and the surrounding country. Tell of Forbes's campaign and the capture of Fort Duquesne. Tell of Washington in the House of Burgesses and of his modesty. Give the story of his marriage. Tell of his non-importation agreement. To what responsible position did the Continental Congress elect Washington ? Tell of Washington's management of the war. Give an account of Washington at Valley Forge. How was Cornwallis captured ? Tell of Washington's farewell to his officers and his return home. Describe his inauguration as President of the United States. Tell of his last years. What kind of man was he ? How has Virginia honored him ?

Geography Study.

Map of Virginia.—Find Westmoreland, Stafford, Frederick, New Kent, Fairfax, and Culpeper counties. Locate Winchester, the Shenandoah River, Alexandria, Fredericksburg and Yorktown. *Map of New Jersey.*—Locate Princeton and Trenton.

* From James Barron Hope's Centennial Ode: "The Arms and the Man."

CHAPTER XV.

THOMAS NELSON, JR.

1738–1789.

THOMAS NELSON, JR.

ONE of the most patriotic men of the Revolutionary period was Thomas Nelson, Jr. He was born in York county in 1738. His father was William Nelson, for many years president of the council of the colony, and at one time acting-governor of Virginia. Thomas Nelson received his early education from the Rev. Mr. Yates in Gloucester county, after which he was sent, at the age of fourteen, to England, where he was put first under tuition of Dr. Newcome, and afterward under that of Dr. Porteus. For a while he attended Eton, and later he entered the famous Trinity College, Cambridge, where he graduated with distinction.

When it was reported that he was returning to the colony, the people of his native county elected him a member of the House of Burgesses, in which body he took his seat when he was just twenty-one years of age. He made his home at Yorktown, and became associated with his father in the mercantile business. On the death of his father he inherited a large estate.

From time to time, Nelson served in the House of Burgesses. He was a member of that House of Burgesses of 1774, which Dunmore dissolved; of the convention of 1774, which elected delegates to the first Continental Congress, and of the convention of 1775, which, at Henry's suggestion, provided for

LUCY GRIMES NELSON.

the defence of the colony. Nelson was made a colonel of the second Virginia regiment, but he resigned this position on being elected a member of the Continental Con-

gress.   We find him again in the convention of 1776,
and here he offered the resolutions drawn by Pendleton
instructing our delegates in Congress to declare the colonies free and independent.

Though Nelson loved England, having been educated
there, he had decided that there was but one course for
the colonies to pursue.   He said: "Having weighed the
argument on both sides, I am clearly of the opinion that
we must, as we value the liberty of America or even her
existence, without a moment's delay declare our independence."   He was again made a member of the Continental Congress and was present on the fourth of July,
when the Declaration of Independence was adopted.   As
one of the representatives of Virginia, he signed that
famous document together with Jefferson, George
Wythe, Richard Henry Lee, Benjamin Harrison, Jr.,
Francis Lightfoot Lee and Carter Braxton.

In 1777, when it was reported that the British fleet
was about to enter the Chesapeake Bay, Thomas Nelson
was elected commander-in-chief of the Virginia troops.
A little later Congress called for volunteers and Nelson
in response raised a company at his own expense, and
marched north to help the Continental army.   In this
enterprise, he spent a great deal of money for which
he was never repaid.   When he reached the North,
General William Howe, the English commander, had

evacuated Philadelphia, so Nelson's troops were disbanded.

In 1779 the English prepared to invade Virginia. Thereupon the Virginia Assembly put the state troops under the direction of Nelson, and tried to raise two million of dollars with which to defend the state. The wealthy men had so little faith in the state government, that they refused to lend money ·to it, but General Nelson came to the rescue and subscribed largely of his own fortune, whereupon many persons decided, on Nelson's security, to let Virginia have the money.

In the fall of 1780, Benedict Arnold, the traitor, sailed up the James River and tried to land near Williamsburg, but was driven off by the militia under General Nelson. Arnold then went up the river to Westover, where he landed some eight hundred men and marched toward Richmond. Nelson, in the meantime, had gone up the James, but reached Westover too late to cut off Arnold, who had proceeded to Richmond and entered the little city. Governor Jefferson and the legislature having abandoned the city, it was plundered by Arnold's troops, and many of the houses were burned. As Arnold returned down the river, he pillaged the country, but for fear of Nelson's troops he retired to Portsmouth. Here the people of Virginia planned to capture the traitor.

A force of two thousand English were sent to Virginia under General Phillips, who occupied Petersburg, to prevent Arnold's being taken prisoner. To meet these English forces, Washington dispatched from his army, then in New York, the young French Marquis de Lafayette, with twelve hundred men. He was joined

BLANDFORD CHURCH, AT PETERSBURG, VIRGINIA.

by about three thousand of the state militia under General Nelson, and attacked the English at Petersburg. Phillips refused to give battle in the field, but remained shut up in Petersburg, a part of which was cannonaded at the command of Lafayette. Phillips was very ill of fever, and while the siege was in progress, he died. It is said that he exclaimed on his death bed, as he heard the roar of cannon, "My God, it is cruel. They will not let me die in peace."

Arnold, who had joined forces with Phillips, now took command of the English, and he sent an officer with a flag and a letter to Lafayette, but the gallant Frenchman refused to have any intercourse whatever with the traitor, and returned the letter unread. Shortly after this Cornwallis arrived in Petersburg and probably saved Arnold from being captured. Cornwallis, being a high-minded man, was disgusted with the traitor Arnold, and no sooner did he reach Virginia than he gave Arnold a leave of absence to return to New York City. Thus departed the traitor from Virginia soil.

Since Cornwallis had in Petersburg nearly eight thousand men, Lafayette did not feel able to resist him, and, therefore, he retired to the vicinity of Richmond to await the reinforcements which Washington was sending under General Wayne. When the British commander heard that he was opposed by Lafayette, it was reported that he said, "The boy can not escape me." But, though only twenty-three years of age, Lafayette was wise beyond his years, and in addition he had the advice of General Nelson. Cornwallis advanced from Petersburg and Lafayette retired by way of Fredericksburg into Culpeper county. A division of troops under Colonel Tarleton was sent to Charlottesville to capture the Virginia legislature and Governor Jefferson. In this Tarleton failed, Jefferson making his escape on horseback from Monticello, and the legislature going across the mountains into the Valley.

Soon after this Jefferson retired from the governorship, and the legislature, almost in despair, elected Nelson as governor. He also continued as commander-in-chief of the Virginia militia, and showed himself worthy to fill both positions.

About the middle of June, General Wayne arrived with about one thousand men to reinforce Lafayette and the Virginians. Cornwallis was then stationed in Hanover, but on Wayne's arrival he retired down the peninsula for fear that his supplies might be cut off, and by the last of August took up his position at Yorktown. At this point, Cornwallis, surrounded by the French and the Americans under Washington, was forced to surrender on October 19, 1781.

Nelson was present at the siege of Yorktown, commanding the state troops. His home, the most conspicuous house in the little village, was occupied by the English, and was thought to be the headquarters of Cornwallis. When an American battery was ordered to open fire upon the house, the gunner hesitated because he did not wish to destroy the home of the gov-

GENERAL NELSON'S HOME AT YORKTOWN.

ernor. Nelson rode up at this time, dismounted from his horse, and himself fired the first shot at his own house. It is said that he even offered a reward of five guineas (twenty-five dollars) to the soldiers for every bomb shell that should be fired into it. Though he had given freely of his money and borrowed for the state on his own credit, he was in addition willing to sacrifice his beautiful mansion for Virginia.

In less than a month Nelson resigned the governorship and retired to private life. The remaining eight years of his life he spent either at Yorktown, or at his plantation in Hanover county. He died in Hanover county, January 4, 1789, in the fifty-first year of his age. He was buried at Yorktown, but no slab marks his grave. After his death, most of his property was sold to pay the debts which he contracted in his country's cause. It is said that even the old family Bible was sold. His state has honored him by placing a bronze statue on the Washington Monument at Richmond, and Virginians will never forget the sacrifices that Nelson made for his country.

Review Questions.

Give an account of the early life of Nelson. What position of honor did he hold? Who were the Virginia signers of the Declaration of Independence? Tell of Nelson's liberality to his state and to the United States. Tell of Arnold in Virginia. Give an account of General Phillips. Tell of the movements of Cornwallis and of Lafayette. Tell of Nelson at Yorktown. Why was his property sold? How has Virginia honored Nelson?

Geography Study.

Map of Virginia.—Find Yorktown, Richmond, Ports. mouth, Petersburg, Fredericksburg, Culpeper county, Charlottesville, and Hanover county.

CHAPTER XVI.

GEORGE ROGERS CLARK.

1752–1818.

WEST of the Alleghany Mountains Virginia claimed, under the charters of 1606 and 1609, a vast territory, which extended to the Mississippi River and embraced the present states of Kentucky, Ohio, Indiana, Illinois, Michigan and Wisconsin. Few permanent settlers had entered this region before the Revolutionary War, though some traders had gone there for the sake of traffic with the Indians.

GEORGE ROGERS CLARK.

Small settlements had been made in what is now Kentucky and Ohio. Farther from the Ohio River in the Northwest Territory, the French made settlements, chiefly at Kaskaskia (Ill.), and Vincennes (Ind.). But the territory south of the Ohio River was always held by the English. Here Daniel Boone had moved with his family in 1775, and here many families also came from Virginia. Among the early settlers was George Rogers Clark.

George Rogers Clark was born in Albemarle county, Virginia, in 1752, not far from the birthplace of Thomas Jefferson.

His father was John Clark, who moved from Albemarle to Caroline county when George was only five years old. Here was the Clark homestead until 1785, when the family moved to Kentucky. In Caroline was born William Clark, who went with Meriwether Lewis to explore the Pacific Coast.

George Rogers Clark received little education, but it is said that he was for nine months in a school conducted by Mr. Donald Robertson, where he was a playmate of James Madison, afterwards President of the United States. Clark, like Washington, was fond of mathematics, and turned his attention to surveying. By 1770, emigrants were crossing the Alleghany Mountains, moving towards the Ohio Valley. Among these was Clark, who took up some land about twenty-five miles from where Wheeling, West Virginia, now stands. Here Clark spent his time in hunting and fishing, and surveying the lands around him.

When Dunmore took the field against the Indians of the Northwest, Clark joined him. He was not at the Battle of Point Pleasant, as he was with the troops which Dunmore commanded in person and not under Andrew Lewis. About a year after the battle of Point Pleasant many settlers went to Kentucky, and of the number was Clark, who soon organized the people into companies to fight the Indians. Through his influence that great western country became a county in Virginia, and sent him and John Gabriel Jones as representatives to the Virginia legislature. Clark and Jones at once began their journey to Williamsburg—through the wilderness and across the mountains—a distance of 700 miles. Much of the way Clark was forced to walk on account of the loss of one of the horses.

On arriving at Williamsburg he found that the legislature was not in session, but he appeared before Governor Patrick Henry and the Virginia Council of State, and showed the urgency of defending Kentucky against the Indians, and at the same time of trying to hold for Virginia the Northwest Territory, which the English from Canada were occupying. Henry saw at once the importance of what Clark proposed to do, and he therefore directed him to raise troops and return to Kentucky. Clark at once got together the soldiers, and when all things were in readiness he sailed down the

Ohio River and entered the southern part of what is now Illinois. There he attacked the town of Kaskaskia, which was held by a garrison of English troops. He secretly entered the place without being detected, walked to the fort and stood in the doorway of the hall watching the dancing. The English did not see him, but an Indian, who was present, noticed the stranger and raised a war whoop. Clark quietly quelled the disturbance and informed the gentlemen that they could proceed with their dance, though they were now prisoners in the hands of the Virginians (1778).

He then went to the home of the commander, Rochblave, who was captured in bed. In the house were some important papers stored in Madam Rochblave's room, and Clark greatly desired to secure them; but his gallantry and respect for ladies was so great that, rather than invade the privacy of a lady's bedchamber, he permitted her to burn the papers without being disturbed.

After this, Clark took possession of Vincennes, whose inhabitants were French, and were glad to transfer their allegiance from the flag of England to that of Virginia. At that time the English had a large force at Detroit under command of Governor Hamilton, who determined, if possible, to hold the Northwest for the English; he, therefore, moved with a large force to the south and recaptured Vincennes. When Clark heard of this, he again collected his troops with the determination either to capture Hamilton and his forces, or to drive them out of the Northwest Territory.

In the middle of the winter (1779) Clark left Kas-

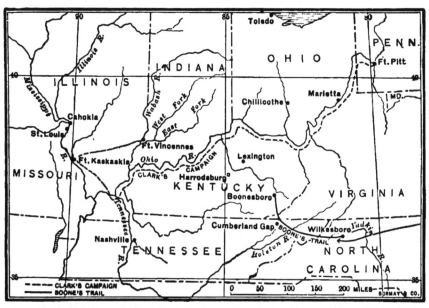

BOONE'S TRAIL (1775) AND CLARK'S CAMPAIGN (1778–79).

kaskia to attack Vincennes. His march was a bold undertaking, and covered a distance of 160 miles through the drowned lands of the Wabash River. Often the soldiers had to go through water up to their waists and sometimes even to their necks. But Clark was dauntless and his men were brave, so they pushed on with determination. Towards the end of the march Clark found the water so deep, and his men were so weak from cold and hunger that he feared to tell them the situation. He then "put some water in his hand, poured on powder, blackened his face, gave the war whoop and marched into the water without saying a word." He ordered his men to begin a favorite song, and the whole force, joining in, marched cheerfully through the water.

After sixteen days of great perseverance and hardships Clark reached Vincennes. His appearance before the town was a surprise, as Hamilton had never dreamed that any man would dare to march from Kaskaskia to Vincennes through the drowned lands of the Wabash River. Clark ordered him to surrender, which he at first refused to do, but at night Clark attacked the fort so vigorously that the next day Hamilton yielded. Clark sent a boat up the Wabash River and captured forty prisoners and fifty thousand dollars' worth of goods and stores. Hamilton and some of the officers and privates were sent as prisoners to Williamsburg. Not only did Clark drive the English from the Northwest, but he also subdued the Indians in that region. We are told that he met them in many conferences, and always succeeded in overawing them. At one meeting he had only seventy men, while the Indians had three hundred. The Indian chief, believing that he was stronger than Clark, placed upon the table, by which Clark was seated, a belt of white and black wampum, meaning that Clark could take either peace or war. Regarding this as an insult, Clark pushed the wampum on the floor, trampled on it and dismissed the Indians from the hall. This courageous act, which meant war, so unnerved the Indians that they at once began to fear Clark and the next day they sued for peace.

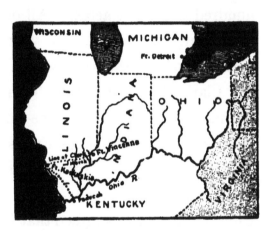

THE OLD NORTHWEST.

Clark, having overcome the English and having forced the Indians to a treaty, now had absolute control of the Northwest Territory. Virginia was delighted with Clark's undertaking. The legislature passed a vote of thanks and presented him with a sword on the scabbard of which were the words, "Sic semper tyrannis," * and on the blade, "A tribute to courage and patriotism presented by the State of Virginia to her beloved son, General George Rogers Clark, who, by the conquest of Illinois and Vincennes, extended her empire and aided

* Thus always with tyrants.

in the defence of her liberties." For their services in the war, Virginia granted to Clark and his soldiers one hundred and fifty thousand acres of land in what is now the state of Indiana. Of this grant Clark received for his part eight thousand acres, and each private received one hundred and eight acres. All of this magnificent territory Virginia gave, a few years later, to the Union.

In conquering the Northwest Territory from the English Clark did a great thing for his country. If he had not made this expedition, the territory would have remained in the hands of the English until the close of the Revolutionary War. By the treaty of peace with England, which acknowledged the independence of the United States, it was agreed that England and the United States should each retain what territory they held at the close of the war. By this treaty, Canada, which was never conquered by the United States, was kept by England, but since Clark had conquered the Northwest Territory this remained in the hands of the United States. So it was through the boldness and bravery of George Rogers Clark that we now have in our union those five magnificent states, Ohio, Indiana, Illinois, Michigan and Wisconsin.

Clark made his home for the rest of his life in Kentucky. Unfortunately he formed the habit of drinking, which prevented him from ever becoming a prominent man.   In 1792 the large county of Kentucky was allowed by Virginia to become a state in the Union, and Clark would undoubtedly have been its governor or one of its Congressmen if he had not been a hard drinker. He died in 1818.   At that time the country which he had seen as a wilderness, had become populous and wealthy.   Already Kentucky, Ohio, Indiana and Illinois were states in the Union, while Michigan, which at that time included Wisconsin, was a flourishing territory.

Review Questions.

What was the Northwest Territory ?   Tell of Clark's early life.   What did he do in Kentucky ?   Tell of his trips to Virginia and of his interview with Governor Henry.   Tell of his attack and capture of Kaskaskia.   Give an account of his march to and capture of Vincennes.   Give the story of Clark's conference with the Indians.   How did Virginia recognize Clark's services ?   What was the importance of Clark's conquest ?   Tell of the last years of Clark.

Geography Study.

Map of Kentucky and the Northwest.—Find Vincennes, Detroit, Kaskaskia, the Wabash River and the Ohio River. *Map of Virginia.*—Find Albemarle county.   How far is it from Albemarle to the Mississippi River?

CHAPTER XVII.

EDMUND PENDLETON.

1721–1803.

ONE of the most prominent figures in the political history of Virginia for the last half of the eighteenth century was Edmund Pendleton. He was born in Caroline county in 1721. His father died a few months before his birth, and young Pendleton, being raised in poverty, had small opportunity for an education. When he was fourteen years old, he was bound as an

EDMUND PENDLETON.

apprentice to Colonel Benjamin Robinson, clerk of Caroline county. Pendleton, however, was ambitious and diligent and he wished to be a great man. What little money he earned, he spent on books, which he read eagerly and carefully. At the age of twenty-one, after a rigid examination, he obtained a license to practice law. At this time he married Miss Betty Roy against the wish and consent of Mr. Robinson. His wife died in less than two years, and, when he was in his twenty-fourth year, he married Miss Sarah Pollard.

Pendleton practiced law in the county court of Caroline and afterwards before the general court of the colony of Virginia, establishing a reputation as a thorough and conscientious lawyer. In 1752 he was elected by Caroline county as one of its members to the House of Burgesses, a position which he held for twenty-four years until the House of Burgesses was extinct and the House of Delegates, one branch of the Virginia legislature, took its place. After two-years' service in the House of Delegates he was made, in 1778, president of the Virginia Court of Appeals, and retained this position until his death.

When, in 1773, on the motion of Dabney Carr, a committee of correspondence was appointed, Pendleton was made one of its members. The duty of this committee was to keep in touch with the sister colonies. The Virginia conventions of 1774 and 1775 elected Pendleton as one of the representatives to the Continental Congress.* Pendleton was also a member of the third Virginia convention in 1776, and he was president of the conventions of 1775 and of 1776.

During this time Pendleton was slow to take steps towards open resistance to the English government.

A VIRGINIA COLONIAL HOME—"WESTOVER."

When Patrick Henry offered his famous resolutions at St. John's Church in Richmond in 1775, asking that the colony be put in a state of defence and that troops be raised for that purpose, Pendleton opposed the measure believing that such action would only increase the bitter feeling existing between Virginia and the mother coun-

* When Dunmore dissolved the Burgesses in 1774 for expressing sympathy for Boston, Virginia suggested the Continental Congress, and called for a state convention to govern in place of Dunmore.

try. At this time he still hoped that the breach between England and the colonies might be healed, but this hope was lost when Dunmore acted so much like a tyrant. In 1775 the convention appointed a committee of safety to govern the affairs of the colony, and of this committee Pendleton was made chairman.

By the time that the convention of 1776 had met, Pendleton knew that the colonies could think of nothing but independence. War was already in existence; the battle of Lexington and Concord had already been fought; Washington was commanding the troops around Boston and in New York, and Lord Dunmore had fled from Williamsburg. Pendleton felt that Virginia should now take some decided stand. He therefore prepared a series of resolutions which were offered to the convention by Thomas Nelson, and which, after careful deliberation, were unanimously adopted. These resolutions declared the colony of Virginia free and independent of England, and also set forth that all the efforts of the united colonies to restore peace had been rejected by the British government, and that the colonies must either submit to English tyranny, or declare themselves free from England and fight for their independence. The Virginia delegates in Congress were, therefore, instructed "to declare the united colonies free and independent states." Another resolution provided for the appointment of a committee to prepare a declaration of the rights and a plan of government for the State of Virginia.

In consequence of the first resolution, Richard Henry Lee moved in the congress a Declaration of Independence which was drawn up by Thomas Jefferson and adopted, July 4, 1776. In consequence of the second resolution, the convention in June adopted Mason's Declaration of Rights and his constitution for Virginia.

When Pendleton's resolutions were adopted, the people of the state went wild with joy, and amid the ringing of bells and the thunder of artillery the royal power of England was rejected and the independence of Virginia was welcomed. Andrew Lewis was then in Williamsburg at the head of the army. Pendleton's resolutions, as adopted, were read to the army in the presence of the general, the committee of safety, the members of the convention and a large concourse of people. The soldiers were greatly delighted, and they were feasted that night at Waller's grove on the outskirts of the town. The city was illuminated with many bonfires. The people did not realize that Williamsburg, where so many governors had lived in royal fashion, was never again to be the home of a representative of the English government. No more governors' balls were to be given at 恥 old palace, no more toasts to the king were to be drunk at governors' banquets. Monarchy was dead in the Old Dominion. The cavalier spirit which had upheld Charles I. and his wicked son, Charles II., no longer had reverence for the English crown, and a democratic spirit had seized hold of the people of Virginia, who were now ready to trample under foot the British lion, the symbol of monarchical government, and to establish a republic in which all the people would be "equally free and independent." All honor is due to old Virginia for having laid the basis of republican government in America by the adoption of Pendleton's resolutions in favor of the Declaration of Independence.

When Virginia became an independent state, Pendleton seemed satisfied. He was in favor of keeping all the old English laws, such as those which united the Church and State and which gave the landed estates to the eldest son. But through the influence of Jefferson these laws were abolished, though Pendleton tried hard to retain them.

While the Church and State were united, the Established Church held many acres of land, known as the glebes. These lands were the property of the State. In 1802 a law was passed ordering the glebes to be sold and the money to be used for the care of the poor. The Episcopal Church, which had been the Established Church, took the matter into the courts, and it came up before the Court of Appeals of Virginia, of which Pendleton was president.

It is said that Pendleton had prepared an opinion in favor of the Church, declaring the law unconstitutional and thereby restoring the glebe lands to the Episcopal Church. The day set for the delivery of the decision was the 26th day of October, 1803, but a few days before, Pendleton was taken sick and died on the very day that he was to have delivered his decision. The new president of the Court of Appeals held a different opinion from Pendleton, so the glebe lands were sold and never restored to the Episcopal Church.

As a judge, Pendleton presided over the Court of Appeals with dignity and fair-mindedness. He showed himself a learned lawyer, and had the respect of all Virginians, even those who held opinions differing from his own.

In 1788 the Constitution of the United States was submitted to the people of Virginia, and it was a question of great importance whether they should adopt or reject it. For the purpose of deciding the matter, a state convention was called to meet at Richmond. All the Union was waiting to see what Virginia would do. Upon her it was thought that the fate of the Constitution hung—that if Virginia should reject it, the new form of government would not go into effect, and that if she should adopt it, the United States would begin a new career as a world power. Therefore, the coming together of the convention at Richmond attracted men not only from Virginia, but from all parts of the Union. When

WASHINGTON, HENRY, AND PENDLETON GOING TO THE FIRST CONGRESS.*

this famous convention met, composed of such men as Patrick Henry, George Wythe, James Madison, George Mason, James Monroe, and scores of other noted men, it is not to be wondered that a great crowd assembled to hear its deliberations.

One of the first steps of the convention was the elec-

*From Irving's "Life of Washington," published by G. P. Putnam's Sons. By permission.

tion of a president, and this honor fell by unanimous vote to Pendleton, who came to the convention as the delegate from Caroline county. This was indeed an honor, when we remember that ten years before this event Pendleton had been thrown from a horse and had dislocated his hip. In consequence he was a cripple, and therefore he was unfitted, in a way, to be a presiding officer. But though he could not rise to his feet to put the motions, he presided with satisfaction to his colleagues. His voice was often heard in debate, advocating the adoption of the Constitution, and his support was of inestimable service to Madison, who probably did more than any one else to prevail upon the convention to ratify the Constitution.

When Pendleton died in 1803 he was mourned throughout the whole state. The governor and council of Virginia wore crape for a month in respect of his memory. For fifty years he had been a conspicuous figure in Virginia history. His reputation as a lawyer was excelled by no man in the state, and both friends and foes had the greatest regard for his honesty, sincerity and nobility of character.

Pendleton started as an apprentice boy bound to a master, but by perseverance and diligence in the performance of duty, he attained many honorable positions. Unlike so many men he never became vain about his abilities, and he always felt that it was only through the providence of God that he had met with success. In expressing thankfulness for what he had accomplished, he said: "Not unto me, O Lord, but unto thy name be the praise."

Review Questions.

Tell of Pendleton's early life. What positions did he hold during his life? What was his reputation as a lawyer ? What was his view at first of the Revolutionary movement ? What resolutions did he have offered in the convention of 1776 ? Tell how they were received. Tell what Richard Henry Lee did in Congress. What did Pendleton think of an Established Church? What was the question of the glebe lands ? Tell of the meeting of the convention of 1788 in Richmond. Tell of Pendleton's success in life. Why did he succeed ?

Geography Study.

Map of Virginia.—Find Caroline county. Through what counties would you travel on horseback in going from Caroline county to Williamsburg ?

15

CHAPTER XVIII.

GEORGE MASON.

1725-1792.

IN Fairfax county, not far from Mount Vernon, is Gunston Hall, the home of George Mason, the friend and neighbor of Washington. George Mason was born in 1725 at Dogue's Neck on the Potomac River, then in Stafford county, but now a part of Fairfax. His father died when Mason was ten years old and, like Washington, his training was left to his mother.

GEORGE MASON.

She devoted herself judiciously to her children, and to her George Mason owed much of his high sense of honor and nobility of character. He was taught at home, and never attended college, though he was a man of culture.

He grew up as a planter and for a while lived on his estate at Dogue's Neck. In 1755 he built Gunston Hall, where he lived until his death, devoting most of his time to his family and his private affairs. He did not care for political office, and advised his sons, " to prefer the happiness of independence and a private station to the troubles and vexations of public business." Therefore he gave his attention to his plantation, which became a great industrial school where the negroes were taught such trades as coopering, blacksmithing or carpentering, though the vast majority were field hands, and worked the wheat, corn and tobacco. From his plantation, Mason made large shipments of tobacco to England.

It was not till 1775 that Mason became an active participant in any of Virginia's revolutionary councils, though he had watched keenly every step of the English government. He often talked with Washington about the state of affairs, and was the author of the "nonimportation" agreement of 1769, and of a series of resolutions adopted by citizens of Fairfax county in denunciation of England. In July, 1775, he was a delegate to the convention, and was made one of the members of the Committee of Safety, of which Pendleton was chairman. This Committee of Safety managed the affairs while the convention was not in session.

When Pendleton's resolutions for independence were adopted, a committee of twenty-eight was appointed to prepare a Declaration of Rights and a constitution. Mason was put on this committee, and to his pen we are indebted for the Declaration of Rights, often called the Bill of Rights, and also for our first constitution.

The Declaration of Rights is the ground work of the government of Virginia. It declares that all men are created equally free and independent; that all power is derived from the people; that government is instituted for the common benefit, protection and security of the people; that no man or set of men is entitled to exclusive or separate privileges; that all men having common interest in the community should have the right to vote, and that the freedom of the press should never be restricted. It further states, "that no free government or a blessing of liberty can be preserved to any people but by firm adherence to justice, moderation, temperance, frugality and virtue," and "that religion can be directed only by reason and conviction, not by force or violence, and therefore, that all men are equally entitled to the free exercise of religion according to the dictates of conscience, and that it is the mutual duty of all to practice

Christian forbearance, love and charity towards each other."

After some debate the Declaration of Rights was adopted on the 12th of June, 1776, and on the 29th day of the same month, the Constitution of Virginia was approved. Thus Virginia became a republic and if we can believe the accounts that have been handed down, George Mason is entitled to the credit of having written both of these documents of which every Virginian is so justly proud.

George Mason seems likewise to have designed the seal of Virginia which represents "Virtue, the genius

THE STATE SEAL OF VIRGINIA.

of the Commonwealth dressed like an Amazon, resting on a spear with one hand and holding a sword with the other, and treading Tyranny represented by a man prostrate, a crown fallen from his head, a broken chain in his left hand and a scourge in his right." Above the head of Virtue is placed the word "Virginia," and underneath the figure the words, "Sic semper tyrannis."

For a while Mason served in the legislature of Virginia, but he had cared little for political life, and declined to become a member of the Continental Congress.

In 1780 he retired from public life. Judging from what Madison wrote at that time, he was a great sufferer with the gout. There were strong demands that he should return to public life, but he positively declined to do so.

In 1784 Virginia had a quarrel with Maryland over navigation of the Potomac River. The legislature of Virginia appointed four commissioners to meet commissioners from Maryland to draw up an agreement concerning the navigation of the river. Though Mason was not a member of the legislature, he was made a commissioner and was placed first on the list. Out of the meeting of these commissioners grew a call for a convention to meet at Annapolis, Maryland, to consider amendments to the Constitution of the United States. The result of the Annapolis Convention was the assembling of a general convention in Philadelphia in 1787.

To this convention Virginia appointed seven delegates: George Washington, Patrick Henry, Edmund Randolph, John Blair, James Madison, George Mason and George Wythe. Patrick Henry declined to serve and Joseph McClurg was appointed in his place. Mason, though suffering severely with the gout, accepted the appointment and went to Philadelphia, where he took a prominent part in the matters under discussion. He did not wish a President, for fear that such an official might assume too many powers. He was the real author of the so-called Compromise plan by which the states were to be represented in the House of Representatives according to population, while each state was to have two senators. Because the convention adopted a Constitution without a Bill of Rights and placed so many restrictions upon the states he refused to sign the Constitution. On returning home from Philadelphia, he was elected a member of the Virginia Convention of 1788, to which the Constitution of the United States was submitted for adoption, and in this body he warmly supported Patrick Henry in trying to reject the new Constitution. In spite of all opposition, however, that instrument of government was adopted by the close vote of eighty-nine to seventy-nine.

Upon the adjournment of the convention, George Mason retired to his home, Gunston Hall, where he spent the remainder of his life. During this period he took a deep interest in politics, and was often consulted by the Virginia leaders. In 1790, on the death of William Grayson, a senator of the United States, George Mason was appointed by Governor Randolph to that responsible position, but he refused to accept. Doubtless his ill health, caused from the gout, influenced him to decline so merited an honor.

He died at Gunston Hall on the 7th of October, 1792. He was buried beside his wife in the burying ground on the family estate. No monument marks his grave. He left an estate of fifteen thousand acres of land on the Potomac and sixty thousand acres in Kentucky, some three hundred slaves, and more than fifty thousand dollars' worth of personal property.

Mason was one of Virginia's great men. As author of the Declaration of Rights and of the first constitution of Virginia he should always be remembered by true and loyal sons of the Old Dominion. He never sought political office, and it was only at the request and entreaty of his friends that he ever accepted public positions. He stands among the most prominent of our Revolutionary leaders because of his wisdom, virtue, and patriotism.

Review Questions.

Tell of the early life of George Mason. Tell of his home at Gunston Hall. What interest did he take in the affairs of Virginia before 1775 ? What did he become in 1775? Tell of the Declaration of Rights and of the first constitution of Virginia. Describe the seal of Virginia. Why did he retire , from political life ? What came out of the meeting of Virginia and Maryland commissioners in 1784? Tell of Mason in the convention of 1787. What position did he take in the convention of 1788 ? Why should Mason be remembered ?

Geography Study.

Map of Virginia.—Find the Potomac River, Stafford county, Fairfax county, and Alexandria.

CHAPTER XIX.

THOMAS JEFFERSON.

1743-1826.

VIRGINIA has contributed many master minds to our national history, and among them Thomas Jefferson ranks first. He probably gave to the United States, and it may be said to the whole world, more broad principles of government than any other one man. Wherever republican forms of government exist, and wherever

THOMAS JEFFERSON.

political equality is the principle of government, there the name of Jefferson will always be uttered with reverence and respect.

Thomas Jefferson was born on April 13, 1743, at Shadwell, near Charlottesville, Virginia. His father was Peter Jefferson and his mother was Jane Randolph. Jefferson's education began when he was five years of age under a private tutor. When he grew older he was sent to a private school. At seventeen, he was ready to enter college. He was a slender young man, thin and raw boned, with reddish hair and grayish hazel eyes. He was not then regarded as handsome, but his face showed great intelligence. When he became a man he was six feet, two inches high. He was fond of shooting and one of the best horsemen in Virginia. Like Henry, he loved music, and as he rode on horseback to William and Mary College in 1760, he carried with him his beloved fiddle.

During his first year at college he studied little, preferring to spend his time at social festivities. Whenever a ball was given in the Apollo room of the old Raleigh Tavern, the young student from Albemarle was sure to be present. After his first year at William and Mary, however, he studied hard, often fifteen hours a day, and is said to have graduated from the college with honor. He then began his study of law under the eminent lawyer, George Wythe, who became the first professor of law at William and Mary College. Jefferson seems to have been on intimate terms with his professors. He dined constantly with Professor Small and Mr. Wythe, and was often the companion of Governor Fauquier, a gay and accomplished gentleman.

Not far from Williamsburg lived a rich lawyer, John Wayles, and with him his widowed daughter, Mrs. Martha Skelton. As she was fond of music, Jefferson spent many a pleasant evening at her home, "The Forest." On the first of January, 1772, they were married and began their journey to Jefferson's beautiful estate, "Monticello," about two miles from Charlottesville. The weather was bad, and before they reached the end of their journey, they had to leave the carriage and proceed on horseback. When they arrived at Monticello, the fires were all out and the servants were away from the house. The dark, snow-covered mountain presented a dreary

"THE FOREST" AS IT LOOKS TO-DAY.

prospect to the young couple; but they were very happy and only joked and laughed at their experience. They went into a pavilion in the yard, and Jefferson found in a bookcase some biscuits and wine, which were the only refreshments that he could offer his bride.

At the time of his marriage, Jefferson was twenty-nine years old. He had been practicing law for five years and had been a member of the assembly from

Albemarle county since 1769. As soon as he became a member of the House of Burgesses, he joined the party that was opposing the British government. He was by nature a bold and fearless thinker, and when a mere boy he had had engraved on a seal as his motto, "Resistance to tyrants is obedience to God," a principle to which he held throughout his long and eventful life.

Jefferson was present when the House of Burgesses passed the resolutions of 1769. He was one of those who signed the agreement not to import goods from England. He was also a member of the House of Burgesses, when, in 1773, it established a Committee of Correspondence between Virginia and the other colonies. Some think that the resolutions for such a committee were drawn by Jefferson, though they were offered in the House by his kinsman, Dabney Carr. Of this committee Jefferson was a member. He served again in the House of Burgesses in 1774, and was one who voted for the resolution appointing a day of fasting and prayer because of the oppressive measures which England had passed against the city of Boston. When the governor dissolved the assembly, Jefferson met with those discontented members who called for a general congress of the colonies and asked the freeholders of Virginia for a convention to consider the state of the colony. To this convention, Jefferson was returned by the people of Albemarle. In 1775 he was elected a member of the Continental Congress. When he took his seat in that body he was a young man of thirty-two, and was already known as an eloquent writer and a Revolutionist.

The following year, there came to the Virginia members of Congress instructions from the Virginia convention that the united colonies should be declared free and independent states; and accordingly Richard Henry Lee, called the American Cicero, moved that a Declaration of Independence should be adopted. In accordance with the motion, a committee was selected of which the members were elected by ballot. Jefferson's facility for writing was so well known to the Congress, that he received the highest number of votes and was named as chairman of the committee over such men as John Adams, Benjamin Franklin, Roger Sherman and Robert R. Livingston. To him as chairman fell the task of drafting that immortal document which stands in the history of the world as the most revolutionary political paper ever written. On the fourth of July, 1776, the instrument, practically as offered by Jefferson, was unanimously adopted and to it were placed the signatures of all the members of Congress then present, except one. The principles set forth in that document mean a government by and for the people, and show that Jefferson

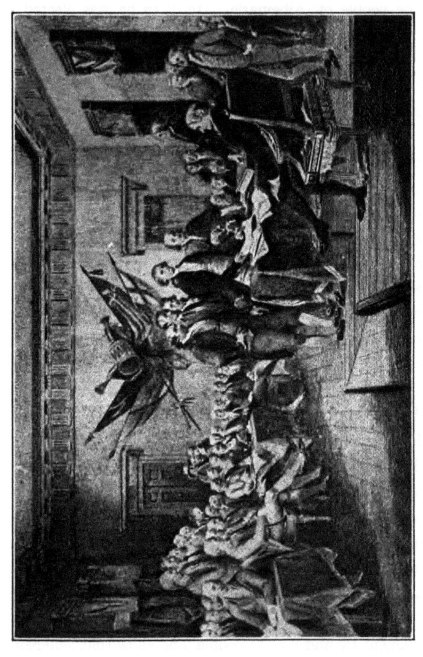

SIGNING THE DECLARATION OF INDEPENDENCE.

was far ahead of his day; for it is only at the dawn of the twentieth century that we are beginning to comprehend the great and universal truths that Jefferson made known to the world.

Jefferson retired from Congress in 1776, returned to his native state and entered the Virginia legislature

MONTICELLO, JEFFERSON'S HOME.

with the hope of revising and modifying her laws so that they might accord with republican government. Believing in freedom of thought he did not see how there could be an Established Church, or how a law could exist whereby preachers not agreeing with that church should be imprisoned. Jefferson thought of those preachers of the Baptist faith who were arrested in Spotsylvania, Caroline, Chesterfield, Culpeper, Orange and Middlesex counties. He remembered how in Culpeper a plot was formed to poison one preacher in jail, and how three were tried in Spotsylvania county, for "preaching the gospel of Christ contrary to the law." Patrick Henry, who was present at the trial, suddenly arose and exclaimed: "May it please your worships, what did I hear read? Did I hear an expression that these men whom your worships are about to try are charged with preaching the gospel of the Son of God?" It is said that on that occasion the prosecuting attorney turned pale. While religious persecution existed in Virginia, about thirty preachers, all told, were imprisoned on the ground that they violated the peace of the community.

In addition to the Baptists, there were many other dissenters—Presbyterians, Quakers and Methodists. At the commencement of the American Revolution, the members of these sects were strong republicans and favored the overthrow of English rule in America. Hawks, in his "History of the Protestant Episcopal Church," tells us that the Baptist preachers advised the young men of their churches to enlist in the Continental Army and in the state troops. The dissenters asked the legislature to do away with an Established Church. They had the support of the more liberal-minded members of the Established Church, and also of the most prominent political leaders of the state. Among the latter were Jefferson and Madison.

In 1776, Jefferson tried to disestablish the Church entirely; in this he was not successful, but only succeeded in securing a bill which allowed all religious denominations to have their houses of worship and all men to preach without molestation. The dissenting ministers were not allowed to perform marriage or funeral rites until 1785. In that year, Jefferson's famous bill for religious liberty, introduced and championed by Mr. Madison, passed the Virginia legislature and established complete religious freedom in the state. Living in this day and generation, when

THE AUTOGRAPH OF JEFFERSON.

everybody has a right to have and to follow his own religious views, it is hard to realize that one hundred years ago no country in the world allowed freedom of religion; even to-day all of the countries of Europe have an established church.

Jefferson felt also that the entail and primogeniture system should be abolished. By this law, it was provided that the eldest son should inherit the landed family estate and that this could not be sold, but should pass from father to son and thus be retained in the family. According to Jefferson, this meant an aristoc-

16

racy, which, he believed, should not exist in a republic. In advocating his bill to abolish entails, Jefferson had strong opponents to contend with, including that wise and eminent statesman, Edmund Pendleton. Nevertheless the legislature passed the bill abolishing the entail and primogeniture system, and thus the last survival of English aristocracy was destroyed in the republic of Virginia.*

Still other schemes for Virginia had this far-seeing Jefferson. He believed that all men should have a voice in the government, but feared that they might give bad rather than good government, unless they were educated. He therefore proposed the establishment of primary and high schools throughout the state, with a state university as a capstone. The legislature adopted his plans, but they were never fully put into operation, and his scheme for the establishment of a university was not accomplished until 1819. He was then an old man and had retired from public life. After various exertions he saw the university established at Charlottesville on broad and liberal plans. He became its first rector, and brought to this country some of the greatest

---

* He was anxious for the abolition of slavery and proposed a plan for future emancipation. His idea was to set a certain year and day after which all negroes born of slave parents should be made free, and should be carried out of the state. Deportation was his solution of the negro problem.

scholars of Europe to instruct the young Virginians. He planned well the institution which was the darling of his old age, for it has not only educated many of the

From a print of 1831.

THE UNIVERSITY OF VIRGINIA.

leaders of our state, but has likewise wielded a great influence over the whole South.

From June, 1779, to June, 1781, Jefferson was governor of Virginia. At this time the state was invaded by the British troops, and Jefferson and the legislature were forced to flee from Richmond to Charlottesville, from which place they were driven by Tarleton. Jefferson lacked the troops and the money with which to defend Virginia properly, though he did all that lay in his power.*

* It was during his administration as governor that Virginia, with the patriotism and sacrifice that should never be forgotten, ceded to the United States that magnificent territory which was hers by charter right as well as by the conquest of George Rogers Clark. Vir-

Jefferson did a great work for his state, but he did much likewise for the United States. He served in Congress from 1783 to 1784; was Minister to France from 1784 to 1789, and was a member of Washington's cabinet, being the first Secretary of State. In the latter position he showed himself a believer in states' rights, claiming that Congress should not legislate about matters which were not expressly provided for in the Constitution of the United States. These views mark him as the founder of what we now call the Democratic party.

After serving one term as Vice-President, he was elected President of the United States and presided over the affairs of our nation for eight years. During his administration that vast territory called Louisiana, from which have been carved the states of Louisiana, Arkansas, Missouri, Kansas, Nebraska, Iowa, Montana, Wyoming and the Dakotas, was purchased from France for fifteen millions of dollars, and thus our dominions were nearly doubled.

On his retirement from the presidency in 1809, Jefferson went to spend the remaining days of his life at Monticello. Here he did not remain inactive, but took

ginia did this for the sake of the Union, for Maryland had refused to be a member of the Union, so long as any of the states held the western lands.

a deep interest in the affairs of Virginia and of the United States. He was consulted for nearly a quarter of a century by the leaders of the Democratic party, and was spoken of as the "Sage of Monticello." He devoted much thought to education, especially to the university. To his home came travelers, tourists, and friends from all parts of the country. His housekeeper often had to provide fifty beds for his guests. Through his generosity and hospitality his fortune of some two hundred thousand dollars slipped away, and, at the time of his death nothing was left save his estate at Monticello, and

Valentine.

THE STATUE OF JEFFERSON AT RICHMOND, VIRGINIA.

that was loaded with debt. He died on the fourth of July, 1826, just fifty years after the Declaration of Independence had been signed.

Jefferson desired to be remembered for three things: as the "Author of the Declaration of American Independence; of the Statute of Virginia for Religious Freedom, and the Father of the University of Virginia" —and these three things place him in the front rank of our great men.

Review Questions.

Tell of Jefferson's early life and student days. Tell of his marriage and trip to Monticello. Tell of Jefferson in the House of Burgesses. Tell of Jefferson in the Continental Congress, and of the drafting of the Declaration of Independence. What were Jefferson's views of government? Give an account of the way dissenting preachers were treated. What was done to the Established Church? Tell of the entail and primogeniture system. Give Jefferson's scheme of education. Tell of the University of Virginia. Tell of Jefferson as governor. What offices did he hold under the United States? What party did he found? Tell of his life at Monticello. When did he die? Write a composition on Jefferson.

Geography Study.

Map of Southern and Western States.—Find Louisiana, Arkansas, Missouri, Kansas, Nebraska, Iowa, Montana, Wyoming, North and South Dakota. *Map of Virginia.*— Find Albemarle county, and Charlotte. Through what counties would you pass in going from Williamsburg to Charlottesville?

CHAPTER XX.

JAMES MADISON.

1751–1836.

THE fourth President of the United States and the third President from Virginia was James Madison. He was born in 1751 at Port Conway, King George county, Virginia, at the home of his mother's father, Mr. Francis Conway. His father was James Madison, who lived at Montpelier, in Orange county.

JAMES MADISON.

At an early age Madison was sent to school to Donald Robertson, a Scotchman, whom Madison spoke of as the learned teacher in King and Queen county, Virginia. At eighteen he entered Princeton College in New Jersey, from which institution he was graduated in 1772, but he remained at college one year longer for the purpose of studying Hebrew. On his return to Montpelier he taught his brothers and sisters, and at this time he probably had some idea of becoming a preacher.

When Madison was only twenty-five years old Orange county honored him by making him a member of the convention of 1776. After the first constitution for Virginia was adopted, he became a member of the legislature in 1776, but the following year he failed to be re-elected. His defeat was due to the fact that he refused to observe the custom of treating at elections,* because he believed that it was wrong to get votes by furnishing whisky, wine, cider, and dinners.

For a while Madison was a member of the governor's council in Virginia, and in 1780 he became a delegate to the Congress at Philadelphia, where he remained for

---

* No man was allowed to vote who did not own at least twenty-five acres of land with a house on it, or fifty acres of unimproved land. On account of these requirements the body of voters was not large in number and the elections were always held at the courthouse on court day, usually in April. There were no ballots in those days, but every man voted openly. The sheriff of the county was the presiding officer at the election and there were two clerks who kept the account of the voters and the man for whom they voted. The candidates for office usually sat in the courthouse on the judges' bench. When a man voted, he told the sheriff the name of the person for whom he voted. The sheriff would then call out the name of the voter and the person voted for. At once the candidate who received the vote would rise and thank the voter. On the outside of the courthouse were friends of the candidate, who dealt out many drinks of wine, whisky, and cider to those persons who had supported or were supporting their candidates. They often furnished the voters with dinner.

three years. On retiring from Congress, Madison again became a member of the Virginia legislature, at which time he carried through Jefferson's bill for religious liberty. He also caused commissioners to be appointed by Virginia who should meet with commissioners from Maryland to discuss the navigation of the Potomac. The meeting of these commissioners showed Madison how weak the government of the United States was, so he drew a resolution which was offered in the Virginia legislature by John Tyler, Sr., calling for a general convention of the states to meet at Annapolis in 1786, to consider changes in the government of the United States. When the Annapolis convention met, only five states (Virginia, Delaware, Pennsylvania, New Jersey, and New York) were represented, so no active steps were taken, except that Congress was asked to call a convention to meet in Philadelphia in May, 1787, to revise the United States government.

When the convention met, Madison was one of the Virginia delegates, and he drew up the plan which was made the basis of our present Constitution. Practically all of the essential features

THE AUTOGRAPH OF MADISON.

were suggested by Madison, and it is for this reason that he is called the Father of the Constitution. The convention, on adjourning, submitted the proposed Constitution to the thirteen states for ratification, with the provision that, as soon as nine states should ratify, the Constitution should go into operation.

Virginia called a convention to decide whether she should adopt or reject the Constitution. Madison was elected a delegate from Orange county, and in the Virginia Convention of 1788 was the chief advocate of the adoption. Against him was pitted Patrick Henry. Be-

MADISON'S HOME AT MONTPELIER.

tween these two a great debate was carried on. Henry's fiery eloquence, filled with convincing power, was met at every point by Madison's cold, logical reasoning, and when the convention voted on the Constitution it was found that Madison had won the victory by the narrow majority of ten.

When the United States government was organized in 1789, under the present Constitution, Madison was a candidate for senator, but Patrick Henry's influence defeated him; however, he ran for the

Hóuse of Representatives and was elected over James Monroe.

After six years in Congress Madison went to live at Montpelier,* where he spent his time looking after his plantation. He studied the best methods of farming and made addresses to farmers' institutes. Farming in Virginia was at a very low state in 1800, and Jefferson, Madison, and John Taylor of Caroline did much to improve it.

When John Adams of Massachusetts was President, the Federalists carried through Congress the Alien and Sedition laws. Under the Alien law, any foreigner who was found in this country and was thought to be a suspicious character might be sent out of the United States at the will of the President. Under the Sedition law, any editor of a newspaper who criticised severely the President or the government might be arrested. These laws created a storm of indignation in the country, and especially in the South. The Jeffersonian party claimed that Congress had no right to pass such laws and that they were unconstitutional. The legislature of Kentucky adopted some resolutions, written by Jefferson, formally declaring that Congress had no right to pass these laws. Resolutions of the same kind, drawn by

* About this time he married Mrs. Dolly Todd. It is interesting to note that Washington and Jefferson also married widows.

Madison, were introduced into the Virginia legislature by John Taylor of Caroline, and, after a warm debate, were adopted. These were the famous Virginia resolutions of 1798. They declared the Alien and Sedition laws unconstitutional and appealed to all the states to do likewise.

At once the country became aroused and the Federalists began to make it appear that the Southern states were trying to break up the Union, but Madison said that his idea was to strengthen the Union by preventing a violation of the Constitution. In order to defend his position, Madison became a candidate for the legislature from Orange county; he was elected a member for the session 1799–1800, and carried through the general assembly what is known as "Madison's Report." The report declared that there was no purpose to destroy the Union, and that, if Congress would hold strictly to the Constitution, the Union would not be dissolved. As we look back to-day we feel that, if Congress had adhered strictly to the Constitution of the United States, according to Madison's wish, many of the troubles which afterward arose in the United States would have been avoided, and possibly the great War between the States would not have occurred.

In 1801 Jefferson became President of the United States. He at once called Madison, who had been his close friend for many years, to be Secretary of State, a post which Madison for eight years filled with credit to himself and with honor to his country. During this whole time he was in perfect harmony with Jefferson, and when the latter retired from the Presidency, he nominated Madison as his successor. From 1809 to 1817 Madison was President of the United States. During this time a second war was fought against Eng-

THE UNIVERSITY OF VIRGINIA AS IT LOOKS TO-DAY.

land, and Madison so greatly increased the power of the United States that he left the White House having the respect of the whole country.

For nineteen years he lived at Montpelier, spending the rest of his life as a Virginia planter and gentleman, but never idle. Along with Jefferson and Monroe he was a member of the Board of Visitors of the University of Virginia, and these three ex-Presidents by their work and their names made the University the great institution that it is. When Jefferson died in 1826, Madison became the Chancellor of the University.

In 1829, after years of controversy, Virginia called a constitutional convention to revise the constitution of 1776. It is an interesting fact that the first resolution ever introduced in the Virginia legislature to revise the state constitution was offered by Madison in 1784, and that forty-five years later the people of Orange sent him to represent them in making a new constitution. Having been in the Virginia convention of 1776, and in the Federal convention of 1787, he was looked upon as a sort of oracle, though he was too old to engage actively in debate. On one occasion, when he rose to speak, the whole house crowded around him to hear the words that fell from his lips. His voice was so weak that his speech could not be heard ten steps away from him. At this time he was seventy-nine years old and was one of the few members of the convention who kept the old style of dress. He wore knee trousers and silk stockings, a stock and a powdered wig.

He lived six years longer and died at Montpelier, on the 28th of June, 1836, at the advanced age of eighty-

five. His death was mourned throughout the United
States. He was a man of broad learning and scholarship, and in his early days a vigorous debater. He was,
moreover, the only one of our great leaders whose private
or public life has not been assailed, and his name will go
down through the ages as that of an honorable, noble
and upright man. He not only would not acquire votes
by treating on election day, but he was one of the few
temperance men of his day. It is said that Madison
never drank a quart of brandy in his whole life, and that
at public dinners where wine was always served, he
rarely partook of it. "Madison was one of the best
men that ever lived."

Review Questions.

Tell of the early life and education of Madison. Tell of his
election to the convention of 1776 and his failure to be elected to
the legislature in 1777. Give an account of what Madison had
to do with calling a convention to draw up the Constitution of
the United States. Why is Madison called the Father of the
Constitution? Tell of Madison in the convention of 1788. What
interest did Madison take in farming? What was his attitude
to the Alien and Sedition laws? What position did he hold
under Jefferson? Tell of his Presidency. Tell of his later
years at Montpelier. Give an account of Madison in the convention of 1829–1830. What kind of man was Madison?

Geography Study.

Map of Virginia.—Find Orange, King George and King
and Queen counties. *Map of New Jersey.*—Find Princeton.

CHAPTER XXI.

JAMES MONROE.

1758-1831.

THE fifth President of the United States and the fourth great Viriginian to hold that position was James Monroe.

He was born in 1758 in Westmoreland county, not far from the birthplace of George Washington. James Monroe first studied under the Rev. Mr. Campbell in Westmoreland, and afterwards entered William and Mary College, then the best institution in America. When the Revolution came on, Monroe was one of the young students who volunteered and entered the army. He soon became a lieutenant and was with Washington at all the battles in New York and New Jersey.

At the battle of Trenton he greatly distinguished himself. The English were endeavoring to form a six-gun battery at the head of King street, when Lieutenant Monroe and Captain William Washington rushed forward with the advance guard and drove the British back and seized two pieces of artillery. For his gallantry Monroe was promoted to a captaincy, and later to a lieutenant-colonelcy.

(*From an old miniature.*)

MRS. JAMES MONROE.

After the Revolutionary War Monroe began the study of law privately under Jefferson, and thus formed a friendship with Jefferson which was only broken by the latter's death. When Monroe was only twenty-three years of age he became a member of the legislature, and the year following he was sent to Congress, in which he seryed three years. In 1787 he was again a member of the Virginia legislature, and in 1788 was a member of the convention of Virginia which ratified the United States Constitution. When the Constitution went into operation, the first senators were Richard Henry Lee and William Grayson. On the death of Grayson a year later Monroe was elected

17

to take his place and served in the Senate for four years.

In 1794 Washington appointed Monroe as Minister to France. On his arrival, the French Convention gave him a hearty welcome, and instructed the presiding officer to give to " citizen Monroe " the accolad. The accolad consisted of an embrace and a kiss imprinted upon the cheek. France was on the point of going to war with England, and, as Monroe was very friendly to the French and said some things that he ought not to have made public, Washington recalled him in disgrace. On returning to America he did not even call to see Washington, but went straight home, and wrote a criticism of the way in which Washington had treated him. Jefferson remained his friend, and two years later, the Jeffersonian party nominated Monroe for governor of Virginia, to which position the legislature elected him for three successive years.

In 1803 Jefferson, who was then President, was very anxious to buy from France the city of New Orleans near the mouth of the Mississippi River, so that the United States might be sure of the right to navigate that great river. Robert Livingston, our Minister to France at that time, was instructed to enter into negotiations for the purchase of New Orleans. Fearing that Livingston might not bring about a successful issue, Jefferson sent James Monroe as a special agent to France to help Livingston. When Monroe reached Paris he found that Napoleon was ready to sell all of the Louisiana Territory, so he and Livingston at once signed a treaty for the whole territory at the small sum of fifteen millions of dollars. Though Livingston always claimed the credit for having made the purchase, it is generally thought that the acquisition of the whole territory was made at the advice of Monroe.

Jefferson had great faith in Monroe, and sent him also as an envoy to England, to negotiate with that country, if possible, a treaty to prevent the English from stopping our ships on the high seas and taking off sailors. In this Monroe was unsuccessful, and, therefore, when he returned to America in 1807 he was in general disfavor with the people.

For a while he retired from public service and practiced law in Fredericksburg. He spoke of being a candidate for the Presidency in 1808, but Jefferson preferred Madison and advised Monroe to wait his turn. A year later he became a member of the legislature and the following year was again made governor of Virginia. Hardly had he assumed the governorship before Madison asked him to become Secretary of State, a position which he held for six years, until he became President of the United States.

As Secretary of State Monroe advised Madison to wage war against England. While the war was in progress Dr. Eustes, the Secretary of War, proved to be inefficient and had to be removed by Madison. Monroe was then made Secretary of War and held that position as well as the Secretaryship of State. Monroe had something of the spirit of a soldier. He had served in the Revolutionary War and was usually spoken of as Colonel Monroe. No sooner did he take charge of the War Department than new life was put into the discouraged American soldiers. Monroe fortified Baltimore and saved it from the British. He kept in close touch with Andrew Jackson in the South. According to Dr. Gilman: "The dispatches sent to Jackson had the ring of determination and authority. Monroe appeared at this time in his best aspects; enthusiastic, determined, confident of the popular vote, daring."

"Hasten your militia to New Orleans," wrote Monroe in rousing dispatches to the governors near the seat of war in Louisiana. "Do not wait for this government to arm them. Put all the arms you can find into their hands. Let every man bring his rifle with him. We shall see you paid." Monroe's conduct during this war undoubtedly made for him many friends.

In 1816 Monroe was elected President by a large

THE VIRGINIA CONSTITUTIONAL CONVENTION OF 1829-30.

majority. In 1820 he was reëlected, receiving every electoral vote except one. The story goes that the elector who voted against him did so in order that Washington might be the only man ever to be unanimously elected President of the United States.

Monroe's administration was marked by two things of importance. For the sum of three million of dollars he purchased Florida from Spain and annexed it to the United States, and in 1823 he sent a message to Congress in which he said that the United States would not allow European countries to seize and colonize any part of North or South America. This famous message was the basis of what is now commonly called "The Monroe Doctrine." This doctrine is not a law, as it was sent to Congress in a message, but it has been generally accepted as an American principle, and the American people will be slow to forget the advice which Monroe gave them. While Monroe was President, there was but one party, the Democratic-Republican party, and his administration is therefore spoken of as the "Era of Good Feeling."

In 1825 Monroe retired from the Presidency at the ripe old age of sixty-seven. The greater part of his latter days was spent at his home, "Oak Hill," in Loudoun county. He served on the Board of Visitors of the University of Virginia with Madison and Jefferson

Monroe always took great interest in his family * and relatives, to whom he often gave wholesome advice. To a nephew he wrote: "Solid merit and virtue alone will support and carry you with credit through the world."

While in retirement at Oak Hill Monroe took a keen interest in the affairs of his native county and state. He even consented to become a local magistrate in Loudoun. We can hardly conceive of an ex-President in these modern days consenting to hold such a humble office. Like Madison and Marshall, Monroe was elected a member of the constitutional convention of 1829-1830, and when the convention met in Richmond, much to his surprise, he was elected president of the body. In this convention Monroe was too feeble to take an active part, but he made one speech which showed what a wise man he was. A great fight was going on between the eastern and western sections of the state with regard to how the members of the legislature should be apportioned to the various sections of the state. Monroe pleaded for harmony and begged for compromise and concession. He said that but for slavery there would be no dissension in Virginia and in the Union, and he insisted that all men should face the

* He married Miss Elisa Kortwright of New York, by whom he had two daughters. One married Samuel Gouverneur of New York, and the other, Judge George Hay of Virginia.

situation and try to remove the evil before some terrible calamity should be brought upon the country.

A year later, on July 4, 1831, Monroe died at the residence of his son-in-law, Mr. Gouverneur, in New York.

MONROE'S TOMB IN HOLLYWOOD CEMETERY.

He was buried in New York, but in 1851 his body was brought to Richmond and interred in Hollywood Cemetery.

Monroe was nearly six feet tall, rather firmly set. His face, when grave, had the expression of sternness, but a smile usually lit up his countenance and gave him the appearance of a kind and good man. In dress he was always a plain and modest gentleman. Like Madison, to the day of his death, he retained the old style of dress—short trousers, silk stockings, knee buckles and low quarter shoes fastened with buckles. He was very polite in his bearing and a man of great sincerity.

Jefferson said of him: "Monroe is so honest that if you turn his soul inside out, there will not be a spot on it."

Monroe was never severe in dealing with his political opponents. He always tried to have a good word to say about everybody. A man who knew him said that he never heard Monroe criticise any one harshly, but that on one occasion, when compelled to give his opinion of John Randolph of Roanoke, Monroe said: "Mr. Randolph is, I think, a capital hand to pull down, but I am not aware that he has ever exhibited much skill as a builder." This homely statement of the character of John Randolph is a true one, and well illustrates Monroe's judgment of men. A historian has told us that in the selection of office holders while he was President, Monroe secured more satisfactory and successful men than any President who had preceded him. He thoroughly understood men and how to judge them. For his long and valuable services to our country he should be ranked by the side of Washington, Jefferson, and Madison.

Review Questions.

Tell of Monroe's education. What did he do at the battle of Trenton? With whom did he read law? Tell what important positions he held. Give an account of his experience as Minister to France and his recall. Tell of the purchase of Louisiana. Why did Monroe return from England in disfavor? Tell of Monroe as Secretary of State and as Secretary

of War. For what is his Presidency known ? How did he
spend his old age ? Tell of Monroe in the convention of 1829-
1830. Tell of his death and burial. What kind of looking
man was Monroe ? Tell of his ability to judge men.

Geography Study.

Map of Virginia.—Find Westmoreland and Loudoun
counties. Locate Fredericksburg.

CHAPTER XXII.

JOHN MARSHALL.

1755–1835.

JOHN MARSHALL was born in Fauquier county, Virginia, about nine miles from Warrenton. His father was Thomas Marshall, a planter of limited means, but a man of high standing and well-known ability. John Marshall was the eldest of fifteen children. Marshall's early childhood was spent in Fauquier county, which was then on our frontier, as the settlements across the Blue Ridge were scattering. So his early days were spent in dread of Indian raids and the scalping knife.

JOHN MARSHALL.

When ten years old, Marshall was sent to Westmoreland county to be placed under the instruction of the Rev. Mr. Campbell. One of his classmates was James Monroe. Here Marshall learned some Latin. A few years afterwards he was sent to the Rev. Mr. Thompson, a Scotch gentleman.

Towards the close of the Revolution (1780) he spent a year at William and Mary College, attending the law lectures given by George Wythe, one of the signers of the Declaration of Independence, and also the course in philosophy, given by Bishop James Madison, then President of William and Mary College.

In 1775, when the news came of the battle of Lexington and Concord, the people of Culpeper organized a regiment of minute men which contained one hundred and fifty men from Culpeper, one hundred from Orange and one hundred from Fauquier. They met near the old courthouse at Culpeper. These were the first minute men raised in Virginia. Lawrence Taliaferro of Orange was made colonel, Edward Stephens of Culpeper, lieutenant-colonel, and Thomas Marshall of Fauquier, major. They adopted a flag having on it the words, "The Culpeper Minute Men, Liberty or Death." On the flag was the picture of a rattlesnake with twelve rattles, coiled and ready to strike. Under-

THE RATTLESNAKE FLAG.

neath were written the words, "Don't tread on me." The head of the rattlesnake represented Virginia, and the twelve rattles, the other twelve English colonies.

John Marshall was a lieutenant in one of the companies. At this time he is represented as "about six feet high, straight and rather slender, dark complexion," with "eyes dark to blackness," and "raven black hair of unusual thickness."

The Culpeper minute men marched to Williamsburg and in 1776 took part in the battle at Great Bridge near Norfolk, where Lord Dunmore was defeated by General Woodford. This was the first of war that John Marshall had seen. He was afterwards made captain in the Continental service, and was with Washington throughout the terrible winter at Valley Forge. In 1780 he returned to Virginia to take charge of some troops to be raised by the state legislature, and it was while remaining in Virginia, inactive, that he pursued his studies at William and Mary College. Soon after this, because there were more officers in the service of Virginia than needed, Marshall resigned his commission as captain and commenced the practice of law. He established his law office in Richmond, and in a little while he was one of the best known lawyers who practiced before the Court of Appeals.

Eight times Marshall was a member of the legislature of Virginia. In 1788 he was a member of the Federal convention and in 1799 he was elected a member of Congress. Marshall was very decidedly opposed to a polit-

ical life.   We are told that he did not wish to run for
Congress, and that only at the persistent entreaty of
George Washington did he consent to be a candidate.
Marshall was not a follower of Jefferson, for he belonged
to the Federalist party, which was regarded by the South-
ern people rather as a Northern party.   Because of his
politics, therefore, Marshall was not popular in Virginia
among the masses of the people, who were generally
Democrats; yet because of his great ability, he defeated
Jefferson's candidate, John Clopton, for Congress.

Marshall made a very active canvass, going to various
places in Henrico county to hold night meetings among
the voters.   It is reported that at one of these meeting:
there was a big bonfire surrounded by citizens of Henrico
and that the tall and dignified John Marshall told
anecdotes and danced jigs to get the favor of his fellow
citizens.   Party feelings ran high at this time.   The
very year in which Marshall was elected to Congress,
it is said that he was present at a meeting held at the
theater in Fredericksburg, Virginia.   When his presence
was noted, a strong Democratic citizen of that ancient
town pointed Marshall out and proposed that he should
be put out of the theater and escorted out of the town
with a band playing "the rogue's march."

In 1800 John Adams called upon Marshall to be his
Secretary of State, a position which he filled only a few

months, for in February, 1801, Adams appointed him
Chief Justice of the United States. For thirty-four
years Marshall presided over the Supreme Court of our
country. These were thirty-four years of great importance in the history of the United States. It was a
decision of this court, delivered by Chief Justice Marshall,
which assumed for the Supreme Court the right to declare a law of Congress unconstitutional. The principle
laid down by Marshall in that decision has since been
held by the Supreme Court, and to-day it is the principle
which guides our country. The Supreme Court, therefore, through the work of Marshall, is now looked upon
as the guardian of our rights and liberties. On the
other hand, Marshall as a presiding officer of the Supreme Court decided a great number of cases in opposition to the states' rights doctrine of Jefferson, Madison,
Monroe and John Taylor of Caroline; and these great
statesmen declared that Marshall was destroying the
individual rights of the states and making a nation of
our country.

While Chief Justice of the United States, Marshall
never lost interest in his native state. From 1815 to
1830 there was great desire in certain sections of Virginia, especially along the Blue Ridge Mountains and in
the Valley, to build canals and good roads. The trade of
the western part of Virginia went to Baltimore, so that

Richmond and Norfolk, which should have been growing cities, were practically small towns. It was hoped that by building good roads and canals the trade from the western part of the state might be brought to eastern Virginia and thus increase the wealth of its cities. Marshall was a great believer in building canals and roads, commonly spoken of as internal improvements, and urged these from time to time. He even consented to become a member of the convention which met at Charlottesville in 1828, and which urged that the legislature should do something to make travel and trade easier between the various sections of the state.

In 1829 he was elected a member of the Constitutional Convention, and because of his better state of health, he took a more active part in debate than either Madison or Monroe.

After becoming Chief Justice, Marshall continued to live in Richmond at the corner of Ninth and Marshall streets. The Supreme Court met at Washington, and in addition to its meetings, he attended the United States circuit courts in Richmond and at Raleigh, N. C. There were no railroads in those days and the journey between these two places had to be made on horse-back or in stage coach, or more frequently by private conveyance. Marshall had an old-fashioned gig in which he frequently drove from Richmond to Washington and from Richmond to Raleigh. About three or four miles from Richmond he owned a farm, which was his great delight. He would often rise early in the morning and ride out to his farm with a bag of clover seed on the saddle behind him, sow it with his own hand,

THE RESIDENCE OF MARSHALL AT RICHMOND.

and return to the city. He wrote James Monroe that his farm was one of the great pleasures of his life.

Marshall's chief amusement was playing quoits. He learned the game when a boy. He played it while he was in the Revolutionary army and he kept it up until his death. There was a quoit club in Richmond and some of the prominent members were Marshall, William Wirt, Wilson Cary Nicholas and George W. Munford, and many others. An artist who saw Marshall at the quoit club in the fall of 1829, while the famous Constitutional Convention was in session, said, "I watched for the coming of the old chief [Marshall]. He soon approached with his coat on his arm and his hat in his

18

hand, which he was using as a fan. He walked directly up to a large bowl of mint julep which had been prepared, drank off a tumbler full of the liquid, smacking his lips, and then turned to his companions with a cheerful 'How are you, gentlemen?' He was looked upon as the best pitcher of the day, and could throw heavier quoits than any other member of the club. The game began with great animation. There were several ties, and before long I saw the great Chief Justice of the United States down on his knees measuring the contested distance with a straw with as much earnestness as if it had been a point of law, and if he proved to be in the right, the woods would ring with his triumphant shout."

In 1831 Marshall's wife died, a shock from which he never recovered. In 1835 his health began to decline rapidly, and he went to Philadelphia for an operation. There he died on July 6th. His body was taken to Richmond and buried by the side of his wife in Shockoe Hill cemetery.*

* Here you may see two simple headstones : one marked, "John Marshall, son of Thomas and Mary Marshall, was born the twenty-fourth day of September, 1755, intermarried with Mary Willis Ambler. the third of January, 1783, departed this life the sixth day of July, 1835." On his wife's tombstone you will read: "Sacred to the memory of Mrs. Mary Willis Marshall, consort of John Marshall, born the thirteenth of March, 1766, departed this life, the twenty-fifth of December, 1831. This stone is erected to her memory by him who best knew her worth and most deplores her loss."

Marshall was a very religious man. He was a constant attendant upon the Episcopal Church in which he was brought up. It is said that Marshall never went to bed without saying the prayers which his mother taught him when a child. He was indeed a bright example of that true manhood, which consists in the union of the greatest ability with the greatest virtue.

Review Questions.

Tell of Marshall's early life and education. Give an account of the Culpeper minute men. Describe Marshall's appearance at this time. Tell of Marshall's connection with the Revolutionary war. Tell what civil offices he held. Describe his canvass for Congress. Why did some people threaten to put him out of a theater in Fredericksburg? Tell of Marshall as Chief Justice of the United States. How did he travel from Richmond to Washington? What interest did he take in his state? Describe an afternoon at the quoit club. Tell of his death. What kind of a man was Marshall?

Geography Study.

Map of Virginia. — Find Orange, Culpeper, Fauquier, and Henrico counties. Locate Warrenton, Williamsburg, Richmond and Fredericksburg.

CHAPTER XXIII.

JOHN RANDOLPH.

1773-1833.

On a high hill in Chesterfield county, overlooking the Appomattox River, there could have been seen in the year 1773 a fine old mansion surrounded by a lawn beautifully laid out with winding walks. This was the birthplace of John Randolph of Roanoke, son of John and Frances Randolph. He was a descendant of Pocahontas, and was proud of the Indian blood that coursed through his viens.

JOHN RANDOLPH.

From a child, John Randolph was very fond of reading, and even before he was eleven years old he had read many of the plays of Shakespeare. Instead of spending his time in the enjoyment of athletic sports, he would steal away to an old closet with a book. But we must not think that all of his boyhood was spent in reading, for he loved to roam over the fields, and also liked to fish.

He was sent, when about nine years old, to a school in Orange county. Soon afterwards he went to Williamsburg to attend the grammar school connected with William and Mary College. While there, he would often go down to the old capitol to study his Greek at the foot of Lord Botetourt's statue, over which a large clock ticked slowly and quietly. Later he was a student at Princeton and Columbia colleges. He despised college honors, and whenever his turn came to speak in a contest for them, he purposely did his worst.

Randolph was devotedly fond of his mother. "She knew better than anyone else the disposition of her sad, sweet child," with his, at times, uncontrollable temper, but withal tenderhearted. Her death was a shock from which he never recovered. This great calamity befell him in his fifteenth year while he was a student at Princeton College. He always kept her picture in his room, and whenever he was in Petersburg or its vicinity he went and wept over her grave.

In 1799 John Randolph became a candidate for Congress. There were at this time two political parties, the Federalist and the Democratic-Republican. The former favored the Alien and Sedition laws, and the latter strongly opposed them. Patrick Henry, now grown very old, thought that no state should pass such resolutions as had been recently agreed upon by the Virginia legislature. Despite his infirm age he thought it his duty to become a candidate for a seat in the legisture of his state. John Randolph was a Democratic-Republican and was in favor of the "Resolutions of '98," as he considered the Alien and Sedition laws contrary to the Constitution and the principles of liberty.

March Court day was the time set for Patrick Henry to address the people of Charlotte county. Everyone thought that it would be the last public speech that the veteran orator would ever make, so great numbers of people assembled at Charlotte Courthouse that day. All the students and professors of the college (Hampden-Sidney) in Prince Edward county, an adjoining county to Charlotte, went to hear him. While the aged patriot was walking along the streets, great crowds were thronging about him. A pious Baptist preacher who was present declared that such reverence to any mortal was almost idolatry, and he said to the people, "Mr. Henry is not a god"; to which the latter replied, "No, indeed; I am only a poor worm of the dust."

It was noticed that a tall, beardless, gawky, but go 1-looking, young man was also moving through the crowd

shaking hands with the people. This was John Randolph, the Democratic-Republican candidate for Congress. He had never made a political speech, but now
determined to answer Henry. The people had no idea

From an old print.

ROANOKE, THE HOME OF JOHN RANDOLPH.

that he would dare to meet the great orator, and they
did not speak in a complimentary manner of the young
candidate. Such remarks as the following could be
heard: "And is that the man who is a candidate for
Congress?" "Is he going to speak against old Pat?"
"Why, he's nothing but a boy—he's got no beard."
"Old Pat will eat him up bodily."

When the time came for the speaking to begin, James

Adams mounted the platform and cried out: "O, yes! O, yes! Colonel Henry will address the people for the last time, and at the risk of his life!" The grand jury, which was in session at that time, rushed through doors and windows and joined the eager crowd. Henry spoke with such fervor and eloquence as was his wont, and when he closed, it is said that his "audience wept like children."

It was now Mr. Randolph's turn to speak in reply. At first he stood for a while silent, his eyes filled with tears, but the astonished crowd was soon greeted with such words as none but a great orator can utter. He spoke very respectfully of Patrick Henry, but at the same time replied to his arguments with fiery eloquence. For two hours his hearers stood and breathlessly drank down "every word that fell from his lips." Henry came up and shook hands with him, and they took dinner together that day. Both candidates were elected.

Mr. Randolph was thus elevated to a seat in the House of Representatives, of which body he was a member for twenty-four years. During this time he was a prominent figure. He was not a great leader, nor was he a strict adherent to any party in Congress. On the whole he was a Democrat, that is, a follower of Jefferson, but he differed from Jefferson on many points about government. Randolph was always true to one principle

—namely, that the Congress of the United States had a right to pass laws only on such subjects as were expressly named in the Constitution.

Had Randolph's views been accepted by Congress there would never have been any Civil War. He constantly warned Congress about its legislation. He believed in the rights of the states, and he tried to keep Congress from taking any rights away from the states. An example of his far-sightedness was shown in 1820, when he declared that Congress had no right to draw a line through the territory of the United States and say that north of that line slavery could not exist. He was one who voted against the measure. In after years the Supreme Court of the United States declared the law unconstitutional; in other words, acknowledged that Randolph had been right.

He was in the United States Senate two years, and for a while was Minister to Russia. He likewise served in the Virginia Convention of 1829–1830, and constantly opposed any change in the Constitution of 1776, claiming that it was the best that the world had ever seen.

While Randolph was in the Senate he made a speech in which he violently attacked the character of Henry Clay. He was very much excited and probably did not know how grave a charge he was making against his political enemy. Clay considered that his honor could be upheld only by challenging his accuser to a duel. The challenge was accepted, and a time and place appointed for a meeting. Before the duel was fought Randolph told two of his friends that, although he was one of the best shots in Virginia, he was going to fire his pistol into the air. He said that he had no intention of causing Clay's wife and children to mourn the loss of a husband and father, and, therefore, he had resolved to throw away his shot.

HENRY CLAY.

The two great statesmen met one afternoon on the banks of the Potomac to engage in what might prove to be a deadly encounter. When the word was given, Clay fired at his antagonist, but the shot did not take effect. Randolph fired his pistol into the air. Clay then came up to Randolph and said: "I trust in God, my dear sir, you are untouched;

after what has occurred, I would not harm you for a thousand worlds."

Randolph's health had in the later years of his life become wretched. In 1833 he started on a voyage to England for the benefit of his health, but did not get farther than Philadelphia, where he died on the twenty-fourth of May of the same year. His remains were carried to Virginia and buried on his estate on the Roanoke River in Charlotte county, where many years of his life had been spent. By his will his slaves were freed and provision was made for buying land for them in some state other than Virginia.

John Randolph was in some ways a strange man. He cared little for public opinion and so took no pains to hide his faults or show his virtues. The world in general and his political enemies in particular usually saw only the bad side of his character. They regarded him as an irritable, high-tempered, and unfeeling, though brilliant man, who took pleasure in causing people pain by hurling his "withering sarcasm" at them. He doubtless had many of the faults that he was accused of, but he also had many good traits of character, which none but his intimate friends appreciated. To them he unbosomed himself, and they accordingly knew and loved him.

Next to the death of his mother the blow that cut the

deepest wound in his heart was a disappointment in love. When the English invaded Virginia in 1781, the Randolph family left their home, "Matoax," to go to another estate that they owned. On their way they stopped for a few days at the home of Mr. Benjamin Ward, Jr. Here young Randolph found a very agreeable playmate in Mr. Ward's little daughter. They were both children then, but this same little girl, grown into womanhood, was the one with whom, in after years, he fell violently in love. Circumstances prevented their marriage, and he was afterwards pained to learn that she had married another. This disappointment destroyed his happiness and spoiled his disposition. We should always remember what troubles and afflictions he endured before passing harsh judgment upon his character.

Review Questions.

Where was John Randolph born? From whom was he descended? Tell of his early life and education. Describe the day at Charlotte Courthouse when Patrick Henry and Randolph spoke. How long was Randolph in Congress? What did he think were the rights of Congress? What offices did he hold? Tell of his duel with Henry Clay. Tell of his death. What sort of man was Randolph?

Geography Study.

Map of Virginia.—Trace the Appomattox River. Locate Charlotte county, Petersburg, Williamsburg and Orange county. What are the adjoining counties to Charlotte? What river flows between Charlotte and Halifax counties?   p 284

CHAPTER XXIV.

JOHN TYLER.

1790–1862.

VIRGINIA has given five Presidents to the Union: Washington, Jefferson, Madison, Monroe and Tyler. All the Virginia Presidents served eight years, except Tyler, who served not quite four. Each Virginia President did a great work for the United States. Washington gained for the country its inde-

GREENWAY, TYLER'S BIRTHPLACE.

pendence, Jefferson purchased Louisiana, Madison maintained the national honor by the second war with England, Monroe acquired Florida, and Tyler negotiated the treaty for the annexation of Texas. Thus, in the history of the American nation Virginians were the leaders both in the gaining of independence and in the acquiring of territory.

John Tyler was born at Greenway, his father's home, in Charles City county, Virginia, in 1790. His father was John Tyler, Sr., who has a claim upon Virginia for three important acts. In 1786, as a member of the legislature, he carried through that body the resolution which called the Annapolis Convention, the forerunner of the Federal Convention of 1787. In 1788, as judge of the general court of Virginia, he held that the judges could set aside an act of the legislature if it was not in accord with the State Constitution. As governor of Virginia, in 1808, he secured the establishment of the literary fund for the purposes of education.

As a boy, John Tyler, Jr., displayed great aptness for learning. He was sent to an old field school conducted by a Mr. McMurdo, who was a hard-hearted disciplinarian, of whom Tyler said it was a wonder he did not whip all the sense out of his scholars. Finally, a number of boys, among them young Tyler, determined to put an end to Mr. McMurdo's cruel treatment; so one day they tripped him up, tied his hands and feet and locked him in the schoolhouse, where he remained a prisoner until late in the evening, when a passer-by, hearing his groans, came in and released him.

At twelve years of age, Tyler entered the grammar school, now the model school of William and Mary College, and proceeded from this into the college proper, where he distinguished himself by graduating at the age of seventeen. He at once devoted himself to the study of law, and at the age of nineteen was admitted to the bar. As an advocate he was usually successful on account of his keen wit, brilliant imagination and the ability to detect the weak points in his opponent's case.

When just twenty-one years of age he became a member of the legislature, and it is interesting to note that at that time he introduced some resolutions to censure the Virginia Senators in Congress, because they had voted that Congress should recharter the Bank of the United States. For five years he was a member of the legislature, and at twenty-six he became a member of Congress, in which body he remained for six years. He was a strong states' rights man, and as such did not believe that Congress had the right to legislate slavery out of the territories. When the Missouri Compromise bill of 1820 was passed, allowing Missouri to come in as a slave state, but forbidding slavery in any territory north of the southern boundary of Missouri (36° 30'), Tyler and John Randolph of Roanoke voted against the measure.

On account of poor health, Tyler retired from Congress in 1821, but four years later he was elected as governor. This position he resigned in order that he might enter the United States Senate, having been elected over John Randolph of Roanoke, who then occupied the seat. He served one term and was re-elected for a second time.

While in the Senate *, Tyler's position in politics was what we might regard, in these modern days, as peculiar, but from the standpoint of the old Virginians his position was clearly understood. When our ancestors threw off the British yoke, they did not organize themselves into parties, such as we have to-day. It was not a question of what party one belonged to, but what principle one advocated and what men one had faith in. Tyler held to principles and to men, not to parties. He was a follower of Mr. Jefferson, a states' rights man, and an opponent of the national bank and high tariff.

When Monroe retired from the Presidency of the United States, there was said to be but one party (Democratic-Republican), but there were four factions; one led by William H. Crawford of Georgia, one by John Quincy Adams of Massachusetts, another by Andrew Jackson of Tennessee, and a fourth by Henry Clay of Kentucky.

Crawford was an elegant gentleman, and his views were in accord with those of Tyler. Therefore, Tyler

* At this time he also served in the Virginia Constitutional Convention of 1829–1830.

had favored the election of Crawford to the Presidency, but when that old gentleman had a stroke of paralysis, Tyler was in the embarrassing position of having to choose one of the three other men. He selected Adams as the least antagonistic to his principles, because he feared that both Henry Clay and Andrew Jackson would wish to use the money of the United States to build canals and public highways, and this, as a states' rights man, Tyler did not believe Congress had the right to do. Adams, however, proved to be in favor of high tariff and internal improvements, so that at the next election Tyler supported Andrew Jackson. Because Jackson vetoed a bill on internal improvements, Tyler was friendly to him; but when Jackson proposed to coerce the independent state of South Carolina, because it set aside the high tariff law of the United States, Tyler withdrew his support from the President. When the "Force Bill," giving the President authority to use the forces of the United States against South Carolina, was introduced, Tyler was the only states' right Senator who stayed in his seat and voted against the measure.

Later, when Jackson removed from the national bank by his own authority the money of the United States, Tyler was still more incensed, because he did not believe that Jackson had the right to do so. Tyler was op-

19

posed to a national bank, but he regarded Jackson's action as high-handed and imperious. Therefore, when Clay's resolution to censure Jackson came up in the Senate, Tyler voted in its favor. In 1836 the general assembly of Virginia passed a resolution instructing her United States senators to vote to erase the resolution of censure which had been passed against Jackson. Tyler refused to vote for the erasure and resigned his seat in the Senate, though his colleague, Benjamin Watkins Leigh, disregarded the Virginia instructions and remained in the Senate.

In 1839 a Whig convention was held at Harrisburg, Pa., and General William Henry Harrison was nominated for President and Tyler for Vice-President. The convention contained many discordant elements. Some of the members were for the bank and some against the bank; many were in favor of internal improvements, and some against them. Tyler was known to be a states' rights man, opposed to a bank being chartered by the United States, and opposed to internal improvements, but he was nominated in order to win the support of the Southern states. The convention did not adopt a platform explaining what principles the party believed in. The campaign was lively, and all through the country was heard the cry: "Tippecanoe and Tyler too." The Whigs were regarded as the party of the people, and to indicate their simplicity a log cabin with coon skins tied by the door and a barrel of hard cider in the doorway, placed upon a wagon drawn by four oxen, was seen in many sections of Virginia. The Whigs won a complete victory.

President Harrison lived but a month after his inaugura- tion and was suc- ceeded by Vice-Presi- dent Tyler. Clay introduced a bill to re-charter the na- tional bank, which passed Congress, but was vetoed by the President. At once the cry was raised

JOHN TYLER.

that Tyler had betrayed his party, but it is to be re- membered that Tyler's principles were well known, and that the Whig party had no fixed views and principles, and in the campaign had demanded no pledge of its candidates. Tyler had followed his convictions, as every true man is expected to do.

During his Presidency, Tyler negotiated, through his

Tyler was made a deputy to the Confederate Provisional Congress, and in the fall of 1861 he was elected to the permanent Congress of the Confederate States, but before taking his seat he died, at the Exchange Hotel in Richmond, on the eighteenth of January, 1862.

He was buried in Hollywood cemetery not far from the spot where President Monroe lies. The legislature of Virginia and the Confederate Congress adopted resolutions of respect, in which they bemoaned the fact that the Confederate States would be deprived of his wisdom and experience. The legislature of Virginia voted a monument to his memory, and the members of the Confederate Congress wore the usual badge of mourning for thirty days.

Review Questions.

Who were the five Virginia Presidents? What do you remember them by? Tell of the early life and education of Tyler. Tell of Tyler as a member of the Virginia legislature. To what positions did the legislature elect him? Give an account of his record as Senator. Explain how Tyler joined the Whigs. Tell of the Whig Presidential campaign of 1840. Why did Tyler veto the Bank Bill? How did the United States get Texas? What was the Peace Conference? What was Tyler's attitude to secession? What was the last position to which he was elected? Tell how the state legislature and the Confederate Congress honored his memory.

Geography Study.

Map of Virginia.—Locate Charles City county and Richmond. *Map of Pennsylvania.*—Find Harrisburg.

CHAPTER XXV.

HENRY A. WISE.

1806-1876.

A PROMINENT figure in Virginia history for nearly fifty years was Henry Alexander Wise, who was born at Drummondtown, Accomac county, Virginia, December 3, 1806. His father was Major John Wise, who had been speaker of the House of Delegates of Virginia. Major Wise died when his son was only six years old, and shortly afterwards Henry's mother also died. Wise was brought up in the home of his grandfather, General Cropper. He was a peculiar boy and unattractive in appearance.

HENRY A. WISE.

When eight years old he was taught by his aunt, Miss Elizabeth Wise, who lived about six miles from Drummondtown. "She curbed the wild and wayward boy and first taught him to read." At the age of twelve, he was sent to Margaret Academy, then near Pungoteaque. This was the first high graded school founded on the Eastern Shore. It was established soon after the Revolutionary War and has been in existence for nearly a century. Here Wise learned Latin and Greek. At sixteen years of age he was sent to Washington College, which is now Washington and Lee University, at Lexington, Virginia. At this institution he distinguished himself, being three times orator of his literary society. After graduating from Washington College he studied law under Judge Henry St. George Tucker, who conducted a private school in Winchester.

For a while Wise practiced law in Tennessee, but he soon returned to Virginia and followed his profession in Accomac county. In 1833 he was a candidate for Congress in opposition to Richard Coke of Williamsburg. Wise and Coke made a canvass throughout the district, holding joint debates in every county. Wise made twenty-seven stump speeches, besides having one hundred and fifty "cross-road skirmishes," and since he had a good reputation as an orator, the voters flocked to see and to hear him. Wise took a high stand in the campaign and just as Madison, fifty years before, had refused to treat in the elections, so Wise now refused either to treat or to drink.

At this time he was a tall young man about six feet high, "thin as a rail, of fair complexion with light auburn hair, almost flaxen, worn long behind the ears, and deep-set piercing hazel eyes. His forehead was broad . . . and he had a large, firmly set mouth above a square chin. . . . His general appearance was youthful, and his pronounced features and clean shaven face added to the young look about him."

After a vigorous campaign, Wise was elected by a majority of four hundred and one votes. He remained in Congress eleven years, during which time a movement to abolish slavery was started in the North. Ex-President John Quincy Adams, a member of the House of Representatives, was constantly presenting petitions from the anti-slavery societies. Wise often crossed swords with him, and it is said that in some ways he and Adams were alike, as both of them were impulsive and ready at any time to begin an argument.

Wise was a Democrat, but he was opposed to Van Buren, partly because the latter refused to enter into negotiations to admit Texas into the Union; and together with John Tyler and some other Democrats, Wise joined the party that elected Harrison President and Tyler Vice-President. Wise was always a warm friend of John Tyler and defended his policy as President of the United States. Tyler appointed Wise

Minister to France, but the Senate declined to confirm the nomination. In 1844, however, Wise was sent as Minister to Brazil, where he remained for three years.

On returning to Virginia he began the practice of law in Accomac county. Many stories are told of how he conducted himself among the people of this locality. On one occasion he was at the sale of the property of a

WASHINGTON AND LEE UNIVERSITY.

deceased man. Among the things to be sold was a large egg-nog bowl in which was some sugar belonging to the widow. While she was looking for a bucket in which to pour the sugar, the auctioneer had sold the bowl with the sugar in it. When the poor widow came in with the bucket to get her sugar, the man who had bought the bowl said that the sugar was his and refused to give it up. The crowd at once hissed him and he appealed to Wise to decide the case. Wise at first declined to give a decision, but the man said, "I want your advice, and whatever you advise, I will do," whereupon Wise said, "The sugar is yours. The widow cannot take it from you." The man then cried out to the crowd, "What did I tell you?" But great was his surprise when Wise said, "Stop! you asked my advice. My charges are five dollars," and he walked up to the man and held out his hand, saying, "Give me the money." The man was so confused that he handed the money to Wise, who, walking over to the widow, said, "Madam, this money is honestly mine. I have a perfect right to dispose of it as I please. Take it, and with it buy more sugar for yourself and your fatherless children."

Wise was elected a member of the constitutional convention of 1850–1851, which body is known in history as the "Reform Convention." Since 1800 hard feelings had existed between the eastern and the western sections of the state, because the people of the western part did not feel that they had proper representation in the legislature, and, moreover, they thought that every white man over twenty-one years of age should be allowed to vote. The eastern people thought that in proportion to its wealth the western section was properly represented in the legislature and they did

not believe that a man ought to vote who did not have
some property.

The constitutional convention of 1829–1830,* of
which you have learned in connection with Madison,
Monroe, Marshall, Randolph and Tyler, though it
made some concessions to the western people, did not
satisfy their demands, so they continued to ask for
reforms in the government, and finally a convention
was called in 1850. Wise was about the only eastern

---

* In 1782 the east had only three times as many people as the
west, and yet four times as many representatives in the legislature.
By the time that the convention of 1829–1830 was called, the popu-
lations of the two sections were nearly equal, but the east paid three
times as much taxes as the west, and the representation of the east
was double that of the west. The eastern members would not give
the western members in this convention representation based on
white population, because there were eight times as many slaves in
eastern Virginia as in western Virginia, and many of the western
people were known to be opposed to slavery. In 1831 occurred a
negro insurrection in Southampton county, headed by Nat Turner,
in which about fifty-five white people were killed. The following
year a bill was proposed in the legislature to emancipate the slaves,
and it lacked only a few votes of passing. As a rule, the eastern members voted against emancipation, and the western people for it.
Another reason why the eastern people feared the west was because
of internal improvements. The western people wanted fine roads
built at the expense of the state. Such roads would have brought .
the trade of the western part of Virginia to Richmond and Norfolk
instead of allowing it to go to Baltimore and Washington. Some
roads were built. This difference in views between the east and west
was so great that when the Civil War came on, it resulted in the
counties west of the Alleghanies not accepting secession, and deliberately tearing themselves from the state of Virginia to organize a new
state.

member of the Convention who believed that the wishes of the western people should be respected. When the question of giving the west more representatives in the legislature came up, Wise spoke for five days advocating their claims, and it is said that though the great Shakespearian actor, Booth, was playing Hamlet at the theater, Wise's dramatic speech drew a larger audience. Principally through his influence, the convention finally decided to make some concessions to the western people.*

In 1856 Wise was named as the candidate of the Democratic party for governor. He had to fight the "Know-nothing" party,† which had been formed as a secret organization. This party was thought to be strong, as it had won in several Northern states. Wise took the stump, and from the Atlantic shore to the borders of the Ohio River the people were stirred by his eloquence and the "Know-nothing" party went down in defeat under his terrible sarcasm. He often began his speech with a text from the book of Job, "For we are but of yesterday and know nothing." On the election day Wise won by ten thousand majority.

* The convention of 1850–1851 was truly a reform convention. Every man over twenty-one years of age was allowed to vote and the governor was to be elected thereafter by the people and not by the legislature as under the old system.

† The party received the name Know-nothing because when a member was questioned about it, he usually answered, "I know-nothing."

When Wise was governor, a Northern fanatic, John Brown, came to Harper's Ferry, seized the arsenal there and urged the negroes to rise in insurrection and kill their masters. Colonel Robert E. Lee was sent from Washington with United States troops; he seized Brown and several of his associates and turned them over to the

A VIEW OF HARPER'S FERRY.

state of Virginia. They were tried, convicted and condemned to be hanged. Wise received more than two thousand letters from the North, some of them filled with threats against him if he allowed the sentence against Brown to go into operation, but this did not move him, and Brown was hanged according to the decision of the court. Then it was that Wendell Phillips preached a sermon in Boston in which he compared John Brown to Jesus Christ, and Henry A. Wise to Pontius Pilate.

When the Southern states seceded from the Union, Wise urged that Virginia should stay in the Union and fight for her rights, and that all the Southern states should do likewise, as none of them had violated the Constitution. But in a short while war was at hand, and the Virginia convention had to decide on which side the state should fight. Wise, who was a member of the convention, urged secession as the only course left. Virginia having joined the Confederacy, Wise entered the army and was made a brigadier-general. He served throughout the war with distinction and was with Lee when he surrended at Appomattox.

At the close of the war, Wise had no home, for his place in Princess Anne county, where he had gone to live before the war, had been seized by Federal troops, and all of his pictures, books and personal property had been stolen and scattered to all parts of the country. Several years after, the Federal government returned to him his estate, but it was in ruins. Wise never again became a citizen of the United States, as he would not take the oath of allegiance; therefore he could not vote or hold office. He began the practice of law in Richmond, where he lived until his death, September 12, 1876.

He never lost interest in his native state, which he

dearly loved. Among the first of his utterances after the war was advice to the young Virginians to go to work; to bring people from the North to settle upon those lands which were uncultivated; to develop commerce, mining and manufacturing; to be high-minded and generous as their fathers had been, but to throw aside idle and profitless pleasures. Many years have passed since he died, and during that time much of his advice has been followed. New settlers have come into our state, and our agricultural condition has improved. Our cities are growing through commercial activity, great quantities of coal and iron are being mined in our mountains, and our people are still high-minded and generous as were our fathers.

Review Questions.

Tell of Wise's early life. How did he succeed at college? Where did he practice law? Tell of his first election to Congress. What sort of looking man was he? Tell of Wise's connection with Tyler. Tell the story of the poor woman's sugar. Give an account of Wise in the convention of 1850–1851. Why was there hard feeling between eastern and western Virginia? Tell of Wise's campaign against Knownothingism. Tell of the hanging of John Brown. What did Wise say about secession? Tell of his advice to young Virginians.

Geography Study.

Map of Virginia.—Find Winchester, Lexington, Accomac county and Princess Anne county. *Map of Tennessee.*—Locate Nashville.

CHAPTER XXVI.

MATTHEW F. MAURY.

1806-1873.

VIRGINIA has been the home of many eminent states men, but it should not be forgotten that she has likewise furnished to the world inventors and scientists. In Cyrus H. McCormick, Virginia gave an inventor who revolutionized farming. When McCormick made, in 1831, in his father's blacksmith shop in Rockbridge county, the first reaper that ever cut a field of wheat, he rendered to civilization a service greater than can be truly estimated. From McCormick's reaper have been developed the self-binders, mowers and corn-harvesters of the modern age, machines which are said to save in labor for the people of the United States, annually, the sum of a million dollars. McCormick's invention has been the greatest blessing that ever befell an agricultural people.

The American people are, however, a great commercial, as well as an agricultural nation, and commerce can not be carried on successfully without a thorough knowledge of the sea and its navigation. In order that

20

the best commercial relations may exist between the various countries of the world there should be rapid communication; so to-day we have cables crossing the ocean, whereby in a few minutes we can communicate with all the civilized parts of the world. From Virginia came the famous man, who, by his study of ocean currents greatly aided successful navigation, and by his deep-sea soundings pointed out the practicability of laying cables at the bottom of the ocean. This man was Matthew F. Maury, known as the "Pathfinder" of the sea.

Maury was born in Spotsylvania county, Virginia, about ten miles west of Fredericksburg, on the 24th of January, 1806. When Matthew was but five years old, his father moved to Franklin, Tennessee, about eighteen miles from Nashville. As soon as he was old enough, young Maury assisted his father in clearing the farm, and while not so engaged, he went to an "old-field" school, where he received some elementary instruction. At the age of twelve young Matthew fell from a tree; the fall slightly injured his spine and caused him almost to bite off his tongue. After he recovered from this fall, his father, fearing that the boy was not strong enough for farm work, decided to give him an education, and young Maury was sent to Harpeth Academy, where he did well, particularly in mathematics.

When eighteen, he was appointed, through the Hon. Sam Houston, then a member of Congress from Tennessee, a midshipman in the navy. Matthew's father did not wish him to enter the navy, because an elder brother, John Maury, had been lost at sea; and, therefore, he refused to give Matthew any money with which to go to Washington City, where he was to report at the Navy Department. Matthew, however, was determined to go, so he borrowed thirty dollars from Mr. Hasbrouck, an instructor at the Harpeth Academy; but this sum of money was not sufficient to take him to Washington. There were neither railroads nor stage-coach

lines in those days leading from Tennessee to Washington, so the trip had to be made by private conveyance or on horseback, and it took more than two weeks. Finally, he found a neighbor who was anxious to sell a horse, and knowing that horses were worth more in eastern Virginia than in the

MATTHEW F. MAURY.

mountains of Tennessee, this man lent young Maury a fine colt which he was to sell on reaching the end of his journey.

After a long ride, Maury reached Albemarle county, where some of his kinspeople lived. They received him with joy, and had an unusually good supper on the night of his arrival. Ice cream was served, and as he was the guest of honor, the servant waited upon him first. Maury had never seen any ice cream in his life, so when a dish of it was placed in front of his plate he helped himself to a spoonful of it, thinking that it was preserves, and passed his saucer on. This little story indicates how simple the life was among the pioneers in western Virginia, Tennessee, and Kentucky.

On entering the service of the United States, Maury was assigned to duty on the Frigate *Brandywine*, and was aboard that vessel when it brought the Marquis de Lafayette to the United States as the guest of the nation. The story is told that in those days upon the ship Maury spent his spare time in the study of mathematics, and that often Lafayette would give an encouraging word to the young midshipman. After making a cruise of the world he returned to America, took the examinations of the Navy Department, and was promoted in a short time to be lieutenant in the navy. He early began to write on subjects connected with the sea, and in 1835 published his first book on navigation.

About this time he was married to Miss Herndon of Fredericksburg. He was so poor that the fee to the minister who married him was the last ten dollars that he had in the world. For a while he was appointed to examine Southern harbors, in which work he was engaged for more than a year. He then visited his aged parents in Tennessee, and on his way back to New York was thrown from the top of a stage coach, having given up his seat inside to a poor woman who could not stand the cold air on the outside. Maury's leg was broken at the knee, and as it was set by a poor surgeon, it was afterward found necessary to break his limb a second time, which was a very painful operation, because in those days the use of chloroform and opium in surgical operations was not known. Maury was somewhat lame the rest of his life on account of this accident.

His book on navigation, his report on the Southern harbors and his numerous articles on the improvement of the navy gave him the reputation of the best-informed man in the navy service, and he was spoken of for the Secretaryship of the Navy. This position, however, was not offered him, but in 1841 he was put in charge of the bureau of charts and instruments in Washington, and by his energy and hard work he developed this into the National Observatory.

While in this position he discovered the cause of the Gulf Stream, and drew maps explaining the currents and winds of the seas, and prepared sailing directions to indicate the best routes for ships in crossing the ocean. He likewise wrote the first physical geography of the sea. At the same time he studied the causes of the changes of the weather and laid the basis of our modern weather bureau. His navigation charts aroused the interest and attention of the whole world, and in 1853 an international conference was held in Brussels to encourage Maury's investigations. At this conference Maury was the ruling spirit, and his reputation as a scientist was so generally recognized that knighthood was conferred upon him by the Czar of Russia, the King of Denmark, the King of Portugal and the King of Belgium, and gold medals were presented to him by Prussia, Austria, Sweden and Holland.

While he was making a chart of the currents of the seas, Maury caused soundings to be taken in various parts of the ocean in order that its depth might be discovered. In doing this, he found that there is a great sub-marine plateau across the Atlantic Ocean, on which a cable could be laid without being disturbed by the ocean currents. Cyrus W. Field took up Maury's suggestion, and in 1857 laid the first trans-Atlantic cable. But Field always acknowledged his debt to Maury, for at a public banquet he said: "Maury furnished the brains, England the money, and I had the work done."

In his efforts to increase the commerce of the South

and the Southwest Maury wrote many papers on navigation * and urged the building of a ship canal across the Isthmus of Panama, which he claimed was superior to the Nicaraguan route. Because of the many things which he did for commerce, the merchants of New York City presented him with a purse of five thousand dollars and a service of silver plate.

THE GRAVE OF MAURY.

In 1861, when Virginia seceded, Maury resigned his position in Washington and went to Richmond. Maury, like Lee, had served the United States for over thirty years, and he hated to leave its service, but when his native state called he felt that he must obey. It is reported, however, that when he went to write his resignation he was so overcome with grief, that he said with a choking voice, "I can not write it."

* Maury also wrote a book on the stars and a set of geographies for school purposes.

He was appointed a commodore in the Confederate Navy and became chief of the seacoast, harbor and river defences of the South. In this position he assisted in fitting out the *Virginia* as an iron-clad — the first that the world ever saw—and he also invented a formidable torpedo to be placed in harbors to blow up hostile ships. Toward the close of the war he was sent to England, and was there when Lee surrendered.

On leaving England Maury went to Mexico and entered the service of Maximilian, the emperor, by whom he was again sent to England. Before he could return Maximilian had been overthrown and the empire of Mexico became a republic. At this time a bank in which Maury had placed his money failed and he had nothing to live upon. But English gentlemen, interested in science, at once raised and presented to him a purse of about fifteen thousand dollars. In 1867 he received, as did also the great poet Tennyson, the degree of Doctor of Laws from Cambridge University, England.

In 1868 he became professor at the Virginia Military Institute at Lexington and there he died February 1, 1873. He lies buried in Hollywood cemetery at Richmond.

Maury inaugurated many measures which were beneficial to humanity. In everything that he did he was wholly patriotic and disinterested. In public and private life he was pure, upright and faithful. It is to be hoped that Virginia will erect a monument to his memory, for so great a benefactor should not go unrecognized by his native state.

Review Questions.

What did Cyrus McCormick do for the world ? What did Maury do ? Tell of Maury's early life. On what subject did he write? What positions did he hold under the United States ? Tell of the honors which he received. What was his connection with the Confederacy ? What position did he hold at the time of his death ? How should Virginia honor Maury ?

Geography Study.

Map of Virginia.—Find Lexington, Fredericksburg and Richmond. Locate Spotsylvania, Rockbridge and Albemarle counties. *Map of Europe.*—Find England, Holland, Belgium, Russia, Austria, Sweden, Denmark, and Prussia.

CHAPTER XXVII.

THOMAS J. JACKSON.

1824–1863.

AMONG the Scotch-Irish who came to Virginia and settled in the Alleghany Mountains about 1750 were John Jackson and his wife Elizabeth Cummins. From

"STONEWALL" JACKSON.

this pair was descended a goodly family by the name of Jackson who lived in Harrison and Lewis counties in western Virginia. A great-grandson was Thomas Jonathan Jackson, who was born at Clarksburg, Harrison county, Virginia, in January, 1824. His father was Jonathan Jackson, a lawyer, and his mother was Julia Neale. When Jackson was only three years old his father died, leaving Mrs. Jackson and her three children, Warren, Thomas and Laura, with no means of support. For a while she taught school and took in sewing, and, afterward, against the wishes of her friends, she married a second time. But her husband, Captain Woodson, was too poor to support her children, and so, at the age of six, young Thomas went to live with his aunt, Mrs. Brake, with whom his brother Warren was already living. Shortly after this the boys' mother died.

Thomas could not get along with his uncle Brake, so he left him and finally went to live with a bachelor uncle named Cummins Jackson, about eighteen miles from Clarksburg. Here his little sister also came to live, as well as his brother Warren. Cummins Jackson sent the children to school, where Thomas was studious and persevering, though he never succeeded in any of his studies except arithmetic. Warren was a restless boy and decided to run away from his uncle and persuaded Thomas to go with him. The children, though but fourteen and twelve years of age, wandered across the country to the Ohio River and, having built a raft, they went down the river until they landed on a small island in the Mississippi. There they made a living by cutting wood for the passing steamboats. The island was full of malaria, and they had chills and fevers, from which they came near dying. After this experience, young Thomas returned to the home of his uncle, Cummins Jackson, and Warren went back to the home of Mrs. Brake, where he soon after died from consumption.

On the farm of Mr. Cummins Jackson, Thomas now

proved very helpful.   It is said that whenever he undertook anything, he would carry it through in spite of all opposition; but though he had a determined will, he had a cheerful, generous nature and a strong sense of justice, and was absolutely truthful.   He had the greatest respect for womankind, even when a boy.   On one occasion at school, a boy much larger than Jackson acted very rudely to one of the girls.   Jackson demanded that he should apologize to the girl, and when the big fellow refused, "Jackson pitched into him and gave him a severe pounding."

When he was eighteen, Jackson made application for a cadetship at the Military Academy at West Point (N. Y.).   On receiving assurances of help from his Congressman he went immediately to Washington, and, though his educational preparation was not the best, the Secretary of War was so pleased with him that he gave him the appointment.   At West Point Jackson proved to be a good student, and, though he scarcely made his classes the first year, he persevered so diligently that at the end of the fourth year he graduated seventeenth in a class of seventy.   One of his classmates said that if there had been one more year to the course "old Jack" would have come out at the head of the class. While at West Point he wrote in his notebook a set of resolutions to govern his life, and at the head of them he put this maxim, "You may be whatever you resolve to be." One of his resolutions was, "Through life let your principal object be the discharge of duty."

On graduating, Jackson went to the Mexican War as a lieutenant in the artillery service, and conducted him-

THE VIRGINIA MILITARY INSTITUTE.

self with such bravery that in the official reports his officers spoke of him in the highest terms. For his gallantry he was made first a captain and then a major. "No officer in the whole army in Mexico was promoted so often for meritorious conduct, or made so great a stride in rank."

On returning from Mexico he was baptized by an Episcopal clergyman, but it was not until 1851 that he connected himself with any church. After deliberation he accepted the Presbyterian faith, and was always a faithful church member. He lived a conscientious life and was a great advocate of the observance of the Sabbath. He felt that something should be done for the religious condition of the negroes, so he established a Sunday-school for them at Lexington. In 1851 he was elected professor of natural philosophy and artillery tactics at the Virginia Military Institute at Lexington. As a professor he was extremely conscientious, though he was not so popular with his students as some of the other professors, because he was strict in his discipline and exacting in his demands of the students; yet all the students had the highest respect for him.

As soon as Virginia seceded from the Union, Jackson decided to enter the army. By Governor Letcher he was commissioned colonel of the Virginia volunteers and was stationed at Harper's Ferry under General Joseph E. Johnston. A few weeks later he was made brigadier-general, and some months afterwards major-general.

When the Federals invaded Virginia in 1861, Jackson's troops were among those sent by General Johnston to reinforce Beauregard at Manassas. In that terrible battle Jackson's brigade saved the day by standing firm when the Confederate troops commanded by General Bee of South Carolina were being driven back. On seeing Jackson, General Bee cried: "Look at Jackson. There he stands like a stone wall! Rally behind the

Virginians." The South Carolinans bravely re-formed their lines and the day was won. Ever since, "Stonewall" Jackson has been a household name in the South.

During the winter of 1861–1862 Jackson stayed at Winchester in charge of the Army of the Valley of Virginia. With the opening of 1862 came Jackson's famous Valley campaign. The weather was cold and the roads were frozen, but Jackson moved his soldiers with such rapidity that they got the title of foot cavalry. He attacked the Federals at Romney, drove them from the entire region of the Valley, and returned to Winchester with his army in high glee, though many a man had a frost-bitten ear, finger or toe.

Shortly after this the Federal General Banks approached within four miles of Winchester and Jackson was forced to retreat up the Valley, but suddenly he retraced his steps and on March 23rd fought a fierce battle with one division of Banks's army under Shields at Kernstown.

The authorities at Washington became uneasy and sent reinforcements to Banks, while Jackson also received reinforcements under Generals Ewell and Edward Johnson, making his army about fifteen thousand. Opposed to him were four Federal armies numbering sixty thousand men. Hearing that Milroy was coming from western Virginia Jackson marched rapidly south, then west, and defeated the Federals at McDowell on May 8th; thereupon he recrossed the mountains, and on May 23rd fell upon part of Banks's army at Front Royal, completely defeating it. Banks then retreated down the Valley, and, as he was pursued by Jackson, he crossed the Potomac into Maryland.

The Federals, believing that Jackson had an army of about fifty thousand men, sent reinforcements to Shields, who was at Front Royal. In the meantime, Frémont came from West Virginia into the Valley, and he and Shields were trying to unite and destroy Jackson's small force. Jackson marched quickly up the Valley, followed by Frémont on one side the Shenandoah River and Shields on the other side. Turning around at Cross Keys,* he defeated Frémont on June 7th; then quickly crossing the Shenandoah River and, burning the bridge, he defeated Shields the next day, June 8th, at Port Republic.

This Valley campaign is one of the most remarkable in history. "Within forty days, he [Jackson] had marched four hundred miles, fought four pitched battles, defeating four separate armies with numerous combats and skirmishes, sent to the rear thirty-five hundred

* In this campaign Brigadier-General Turner Ashby was killed. He was one of the most daring cavalry officers in the Confederate service.

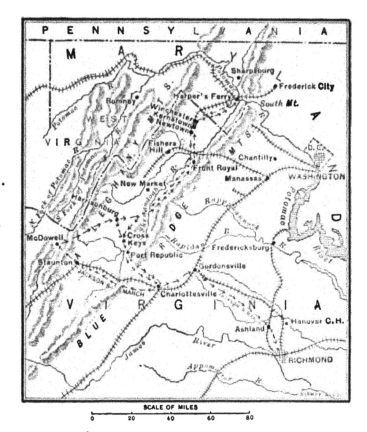

JACKSON'S CAMPAIGN IN THE VALLEY OF VIRGINIA.

prisoners, killed and wounded a still larger number of the enemy," and had kept sixty thousand Federal troops from joining McClellan in his attack on Richmond.

No sooner had the Valley been cleared of the enemy than Jackson took his army to Richmond and assisted Lee in driving McClellan from Virginia. When Lee moved north, Jackson went with him, and was a conspicuous figure in the second battle of Manassas; where the Federals, under General Pope, were defeated.   Jackson now took Harper's Ferry, and, joining Lee in Maryland, commanded the Confederate left in the battle of Sharpsburg.   After this battle Lee returned into Virginia and took up his position at Fredericksburg, where the Federal General Burnside was terribly defeated (December, 1862).   Jackson commanded the right of the Confederates in this battle.

For the winter of 1861-1862 Jackson was stationed at Moss Neck in Caroline county.   He provided chaplains for his army and had meetings held by many denominations.   A Presbyterian minister in describing the services held in the general's camp said, "So we had a Presbyterian sermon introduced by Baptist services under the direction of a Methodist Chaplain in an Episcopal Church."

In the spring Federal General Hooker crossed the Rapidan River and took up his position at Chancellorsville.   Here occurred one of the great battles of the war, and Hooker was completely routed. Jackson was sent to make a flank movement, and on May 2, 1863, he was six miles west of Chancellorsville in the rear of the enemy.   Through dense woods Jackson's men attacked the Federals and swept them from their lines.   All that was needed to put the Union soldiers to flight was a rapid advance of the Confederates.

Jackson therefore dashed among his troops, saying, "Men, get into line! Get into line!" Then he rode out with a party in front of his line for about a hundred yards to view the position of the enemy. Here he was fired upon by the Federals, and while he was returning rapidly to his own lines, his men, mistaking him and his attendants for a body of Federal cavalry, opened fire. "His right hand was pierced by a bullet, his left arm was shattered by two balls, one above and one below the elbow breaking the bones and severing the main arteries."

STATUE OF "STONEWALL" JACKSON.

With much difficulty Jackson was carried to the rear, where he was put in an ambulance, and taken to the home of Mr. Thomas C. Chandler at Guiney's Station. He gradually grew worse, and just before he died he was heard to say, "Let us cross the river and rest under the shade of the trees." He had often said that he wished to die on the Lord's day, and his wish was gratified, for he passed away on a beautiful Sunday in May, 1863.

Jackson's death was a great blow to the Confederacy. He was often spoken of as Lee's " right arm," and many a time did Lee wish for the gallant "Stonewall" Jackson who had never known a real defeat. Throughout life Jackson had made the discharge of duty his foremost thought. He never asked for a day's furlough while he was in the army. In all things he was faithful—to his family, to his country, and to his God.

Review Questions.

Tell of Jackson's early life and education. How did he succeed at West Point ? What was said of him in the Mexican War ? Tell of his church relations. What position did he hold at Virginia Military Institute ? How did he get the name of "Stonewall" ? Describe his famous Valley campaign. At what great battles was he with Lee ? Tell of his death.

Geography Study.

Map of West Virginia.—Find Clarksburg, Lewis county, Harrison county and Ohio River. *Map of Virginia.*—Find Lexington, Harper's Ferry. Winchester, Harrisonburg, Manassas, Fredericksburg and Caroline county.

CHAPTER XXVIII.

ROBERT E. LEE.

1807–1870.

WHEN Virginia seceded from the Union, some of her bravest sons were members of the Army of the United States; but, true and loyal to their mother state, they resigned their commissions and returned home to do the bidding of the Old Dominion. One of the first to answer the call of old Virginia was Robert Edward Lee.

He was born at Stratford, in Westmoreland county, Virginia, on the nineteenth of January,

" LIGHT-HORSE HARRY " LEE.

1807. His father, General Henry ("Light Horse Harry") Lee of Revolutionary fame, died when Robert was a boy, and therefore his training was left to his mother. She was a good woman and raised her son to be a devout Christian man. When Robert was not at school, he spent his leisure time with her. On one occasion when his mother was sick, he took the keys and kept house. He was so constantly her companion, that she once said, "How can I spare Robert? He is both a son and a daughter to me."

At eighteen he received an appointment as a cadet to the United States Military Academy at West Point, and after four years he was graduated second in a class of forty-six and became a second lieutenant in the corps of engineers. While at West Point his conduct was irreproachable, his habits were excellent, and he did not receive a demerit in the whole four years.

In 1831 he married Mary Custis, the daughter of George Washington Parke Custis of Arlington. On the death of Mr. Custis Mrs. Lee inherited that magnificent estate, Arlington, which, during the war, was taken from the Lees by the Federal government.

Lee was rapidly promoted, and by 1835 held the rank of captain. When the war with Mexico broke out in 1846, Lee went with General Scott as engineer. His services were so valuable in planning batteries that in the report of the siege of Vera Cruz General Scott wrote: "I am compelled to make special mention of Captain Robert E. Lee, Engineer." When the campaign had closed, General Scott was often heard to say that his success in Mexico was largely due to the skill, valor, and undaunted courage of Robert E. Lee, who was the greatest military genius in America and the best soldier that he ever saw in the field; and that if the opportunity offered, Lee would show himself the foremost captain of his day.

THE ARLINGTON HOME.

General Scott's prediction came true, but in a way very different from his expectations.* Scott had hoped that the opportunity would come to Lee as a general in the Army of the United States, but Lee was destined to distinguish himself as the foremost man of

---

* Soon after the Mexican War Lee was made superintendent of the United States Military Academy at West Point, which position he held for three years, and the academy was greatly improved during his administration. He was then made a lieutenant-colonel in the cavalry service, and for a time was stationed at Louisville, Kentucky, and afterwards in Texas, where he had to fight against the Comanche Indians. In 1859 he was at home on a furlough when the John Brown raid occurred. The Secretary of War at once sent across the Potomac River to Lee's beautiful home, Arlington, and asked him to go to Harper's Ferry to capture John Brown.

his age in the war against the United States. Lee never advocated secession, and, therefore, it was a great blow to him when his native state, Virginia, decided to leave the Union, but he never hesitated about obeying her call.

For thirty-two years Lee had served in the Army of the United States, and it was a struggle for him to leave its services; but he never failed to do what he thought was his duty, and, although President Lincoln offered to put him in command of the active army of the United States, he declined the high compliment and sent in his resignation to the War Department of the United States. At the same time he wrote a letter to General Winfield Scott, then commander-in-chief of the army, in which he said, "Save in the defense of my native state, I never desire again to draw my sword." But Virginia at once called upon her great son, and he was made commander-in-chief of the Virginia forces.

In obedience to the call of his state he went to Richmond to take command of the Virginia forces. The Virginia secession convention was then in session, and an invitation was sent to him to appear before it. When he entered the hall, he was welcomed by Mr. Janney, the presiding officer, who closed his speech by saying: "Yesterday your mother Virginia placed her sword in your hands upon the implied condition that in all things you will keep it to the letter and spirit, that you will draw it only in defence, and that you will fall with it in your hand, rather than the object for which it is placed there should fail."

General Lee could hardly reply on account of his modesty, but finally he said, "Mr. President and gentlemen of the convention, I accept the position assigned me by your partiality. I would have much preferred that the choice would have fallen upon an abler man. Trusting in Almighty God and approving conscience, and the aid of my fellow citizens, I devote myself to the services of my native state, in whose behalf alone I will ever again draw my sword." This was Lee's first and last speech.

Not long after this, war began in real earnest. In the middle of the summer of 1861, the Confederates defeated the Federals at Bull Run, near Manassas, Virginia, and the invasion of Virginia was checked. At this time Lee was in Richmond, where he was detained by President Davis. A little later Lee was sent to western Virginia to command the Confederate forces, and in this section he was not so successful as his friends had expected. The trouble lay not with Lee, but in the fact that he did not have forces enough to manage the difficult situation in western Virginia.

In 1862 his opportunity came. Gen. George B. McClellan, with a strong Union army undertook to advance

from Yorktown against Richmond, but found himself
opposed by Gen. Joseph E. Johnston.   In the battle
that ensued Johnston was wounded, and General Lee,
on the first of June, was put in command of the Army

JOSEPH E. JOHNSTON.

of Northern Virginia, which
command he retained until
the surrender at Appo-
mattox.

After seven days' fight-
ing McClellan was driven
back.   Operations against
Richmond were given up
for the time being, and the
South became jubilant and
the North despondent. Lee
marched north and de-
feated the Federals under
General Pope at the second

battle of Manassas, pushed into Maryland, and fought
the battle of Antietam, or Sharpsburg, and then retired
into Virginia.   In December of the same year (1862) he
terribly defeated Burnside at Fredericksburg, Va.

In May, 1863, Lee inflicted even a worse defeat upon
General Hooker at Chancellorsville, a short distance
from Fredericksburg. The battle of Chancellorsville
was a costly one to the Confederates, on account of the

loss of General "Stonewall" Jackson. Lee then marched into the North; crossed Maryland and entered Pennsylvania; but at Gettysburg he was stopped by the Federals under General Meade. Here was fought a three-days' battle. On the last day the Confederates under General Pickett made a heroic charge against the Federal center, but were compelled to withdraw. As they came back, Lee rode out to meet them. He encouraged the men and said to them: "All this has been my fault and it is I who have lost the fight. You must help me out as best you can." He was brave in victory, but braver in defeat. He never tried to place the responsibility of the defeat upon another, but took it all upon himself.

In March, 1864, General U. S. Grant, who had distinguished himself in some campaigns along the Mississippi River, was appointed Commander-in-Chief of the Army of the Potomac, then stationed in northern Virginia, and began to advance toward Richmond. For a little over a year, a terrible campaign went on between Lee and Grant. It began with the battle of the Wilderness in Spotsylvania county, Virginia, and ended with the surrender of Lee at Appomattox Courthouse. Lee did all that any man could do to prevent defeat, but Grant's army greatly outnumbered his. Grant often had five times as many soldiers as Lee, and he, therefore, adopted the hammering process, that is, kept on fighting and fighting, it mattered not how many troops he lost. Grant had a wagon train that would have reached on a single road from Fredericksburg to Richmond, a distance of sixty-five miles. He had unlimited resources, splendid guns and immense quantities of provisions for his troops.

The first battle of 1864 was fought in the Wilderness, where Grant was severely repulsed, his loss amounting to seventeen thousand men. Lee fell back to Spotsylvania Courthouse, fifteen miles from the Wilderness, and there occurred another desperate engagement. Gradually, Lee was pushed back from Spotsylvania Courthouse toward Richmond, but he stubbornly contested every inch of ground as he retired. At Cold Harbor Lee stood like a rock against Grant, who made a desperate effort to break the Confederate lines. Lee's troops were angry and hungry, for they had had nothing but three hard biscuits and one piece of fat pork apiece for a day's rations.* When the Federals advanced on the hungry Confederates they met with a destructive fire, which in ten minutes caused 12,737 of the Union soldiers to fall, either killed or wounded.

* It is said that one poor fellow had his cracker shot out of his hand before he could eat it, at which he said, "The next time I'll put my cracker in a safe place down by the breastworks where it won't get wounded."

Grant now determined to cross the James River and to attack Petersburg. Then it was that Lee had to retire into Petersburg and Richmond and entrench himself. Here he remained throughout the hard winter of

ROBERT E. LEE.

1864–1865, during which time his troops suffered terribly, and often his soldiers had nothing to eat but parched corn. Confederate money was worthless. Flour was valued at from two to three hundred dollars a barrel, corn forty dollars a barrel, sugar ten dollars per pound, and calico thirty dollars per yard.

Lee tried to maintain his lines which stretched over a distance of forty miles, but on account of starvation and sickness his army grew smaller and smaller, and at last, in April, 1865, he was forced to

abandon Petersburg and Richmond. He wished to go
South and unite with General Johnston in North Carolina, but, on reaching Amelia Courthouse, he found
Grant in front of him; so he turned westward hoping
to reach Lynchburg, but at Appomattox Courthouse
he again found that Grant had blocked his way.
Thereupon he sent a note to Grant requesting an interview with reference to the surrender of the army.
They met at the house of Mr. Wilmer McLean at Appomattox Courthouse at one o'clock on the ninth of
April, 1865.

It was a sad day for Lee and it was undoubtedly the
greatest struggle of his life to meet Grant to arrange
the terms. Since the soldiers were willing to lay down
their lives rather than surrender, it took greater courage
to submit than to die on the battlefield. Lee felt,
however, that it was useless to waste human life in a
vain effort, and, as in all other things, he had followed
the call of duty, so now, realizing that the overthrow
of the Confederacy was inevitable, he believed that the
true and proper course was to surrender his army.

When Lee and Grant met at Appomattox, there was
a great contrast between the two men. Lee was fifty-
eight years of age, with gray hair and beard, while
Grant was only forty-three, in the very prime of life.
Lee conducted himself with great dignity. He and

Grant had met once before, both having fought in the Mexican War.

As quickly as possible the terms of surrender were arranged. The Confederate soldiers were allowed to return home, with the understanding that they were not again to bear arms against the United States. Grant allowed each soldier to carry home a horse or a mule, if he claimed it was his own property. On learning from Lee that the Southern soldiers had been living for the last few days on parched corn, Grant immediately ordered Lee to be furnished with rations for twenty-five thousand men. Grant was very courteous in his conduct to Lee. He did not take Lee's sword, and he afterwards recommended to the United States government that Lee should be pardoned. General Lee always said: "No man could have behaved better than General Grant did under the circumstances."

When Lee rode from Appomattox Courthouse he was met by his soldiers anxiously awaiting the news of his interview with Grant. On being told that the war was over, and that their beloved Confederacy was at an end, many a brave and hardy soldier broke down and sobbed like a child.

They pressed around him, eager to touch his person or his horse. He turned to his men and said:

"Men, we have fought through the war together; I have done my best for you; my heart is too full to say more." The next day he issued a farewell address to the Army of Northern Virginia and closed it with these words: "By the terms of agreement, officers and men can return to their homes and remain there until exchanged. You will take with you the satisfaction that proceeds from the consciousness of

duty well performed, and I earnestly pray that a merciful God will extend to you his blessing and protection. With an unceasing ad-

LEE'S STUDY AT LEXINGTON.

miration of your constancy and devotion to your country, and the grateful remembrance of your kind and generous consideration of myself, I bid you an affectionate farewell."

Lee now retired to private life, but was soon afterward made president of Washington College at Lexington, Virginia, now Washington and Lee University. For five years he served the institution faithfully; and, *though* *offered* many positions which would have paid him large sums of money, he refused them all.

He died October the twelfth, 1870. During his last illness his thoughts turned to the battlefield and in death's delirium he was heard to say, "Tell Hill he must come up." He was buried in the chapel of Washington and Lee University. Lee was conscientious and faithful, and "duty" was his watchword. His virtues will live forever, and his character will be imitated by generations yet unborn.

At Washington and Lee University a beautiful recumbent statue has been erected to Lee's memory, and at Richmond stands a magnificent monument which represents Lee

THE LEE STATUE AT RICHMOND.

on his war horse, "Traveler." When the cornerstone of the Lee Monument in Richmond was laid, a beautiful ode written by James Barron Hope was read. The closing stanzas are:

22

" Our past is full of glories,
　　It is a shut-in sea.
The pillars overlooking it
　　Are Washington and Lee,
And a future spreads before us,
　　Not unworthy of the free.

" And here and now, my countrymen,
　　Upon this sacred sod,
Let us feel: It was ' Our Father '
　　Who above us held the rod,
And from hills to sea,
　　Like Robert Lee,
Bow reverently to God."

Review Questions.

Tell of the early life of Lee. What kind of student was Lee at West Point? Tell of his service in Mexico. What did Scott say of him? Tell what positions he held in the service of the United States. Why did Lee resign from the United States Army? Tell of his reception before the Virginia convention. What was the result of his campaign in West Virginia? Outline the campaign of 1862. Give a summary of the campaign of 1863. Tell of the struggle between Lee and Grant. Tell of Lee's surrender at Appomattox. Tell of Lee's farewell to his army. How did Lee spend the last days of his life? Quote from Hope's ode on Lee.

Geography Study.

Map of Virginia.—Find Westmoreland county, Fredericksburg, Petersburg, Richmond, Spotsylvania Courthouse, Appomattox Courthouse, Amelia Courthouse, Lynchburg. *Maps of Maryland and Pennsylvania.*—Find Sharpsburg (Md.) and Gettysburg (Pa.).

CHAPTER XXIX.

WILLIAM HENRY RUFFNER.

1824———.

THE War between the States left Virginia in ruin. Her homes were desolate, for there were few families that had not lost one or more of their members in the terrible struggle. All the energies of our people having been bent upon their great fight for liberty, the farms had been neglected, and many of the best plantations were in a poor state of cultivation. Labor was hard to secure because of the Freedmen's Bureau established by Congress, which so demoralized the negroes that they would not work. Moreover, the poor Confederate soldier, when he returned from Appomattox, had no money with which to employ laborers. The task that lay before the Virginians looked hopeless, but we are proud of our people, because out of chaos they have brought order, and out of ruin they have produced wealth.

At once the planters began as rapidly as possible to improve their farms, while many of the younger men went to the towns and found work there in the manu-

facturing enterprises which were being established.
Richmond had only 37,000 people in 1860, but because
of its increase of manufacturing enterprises it had a

A DESERTED PLANTATION AFTER THE WAR.

population of 51,000 in 1870, and other towns were
growing in like proportion.

For the first five years after the war our development
was somewhat held back by the efforts of the Congress
of the United States to take the government of the state
out of the hands of the native Virginians and to put it
into the hands of negroes and Northern incomers (the
"Carpet Baggers") and some few native whites called
"Scallawags."

Under the acts of Congress (1867) Virginia was put under military rule, and General Schofield was put in charge of the military district. He called a constitutional convention which met in Richmond in 1867, composed of one hundred and five members, of whom twenty-four were negroes, fourteen "Scallawags," and thirty "Carpet Baggers." This convention drew up a constitution with the expressed purpose of taking the government away from those Virginians who had fought for their state. By its provisions no man should vote who had previous to the war held office of any kind, and who had afterwards fought for or aided the Confederacy. This is known as the "disfranchising clause." But the convention went further, and declared that every man who should be elected to office must take an oath that he had never helped the Confederacy in any way. This is known as the "iron-clad" oath, and because of it ninety-nine out of every hundred native white Virginians could not have held office.

When the constitution was submitted to the people of Virginia for ratification, General Grant, then President of the United States, kindly set aside the "disfranchising clause" and the "iron-clad" oath to be voted on separately. The best element of Virginia, aided by the more honorable Northerners who had come to Virginia, succeeded in defeating these two clauses, while the rest of the constitution was ratified (1869), and the following year Virginia was readmitted as a state in the Union. At once the government of Virginia passed into the hands

STRIPPING THE TOBACCO LEAF, AN INDUSTRIAL SCENE IN VIRGINIA TO-DAY.

of the whites, and since that time our state has rapidly progressed.*

With the two objectionable clauses removed, the

* Virginia came out of the war with a large debt, but after years of controversy the matter was settled during the administration of Governor McKinney, and the credit of our State is now good and there is a large surplus in the state treasury. At present the crying need of the country districts is good public highways, and influential men are earnestly working that the roads may be improved.

constitution of 1867 was not such a bad instrument of government, and it remained in force in our state till 1902, when Virginia held another constitutional convention, of which the Hon. John Goode was president. Our last convention modified somewhat the form of government, so that its burdens might be more equally distributed among all classes of people.

The constitution of 1867 provided for the establishment of a public school system, which was put into operation by Dr. William Henry Ruffner as the first Superintendent of Public Instruction.

Dr. Ruffner was born at Lexington, Va., in 1824. He was educated at Washington College, now Washington and Lee University, from which institution he was graduated with the Master of Arts degree. He continued his studies at the Union Theological Seminary, at Hampden-Sidney and under Dr. W. H. McGuffey at the University of Virginia, after which he studied theology at Princeton and entered the Presbyterian ministry. For two years he was chaplain at the University of Virginia, and afterwards pastor of the Seventh Presbyterian Church, Philadelphia, which position he resigned on account of ill health. He returned to Virginia in 1853 and resorted to farming for his health.

In 1870 he was elected by the legislature Superintend-

ent of Public Instruction over fifteen applicants.*   At
this time, Virginia had no public schools open to all the
children of the state, though since 1808, by the establishment of the Literary Fund of Virginia, some pro-

DR. WILLIAM H. RUFFNER.

visions had been made for
the education of the poor.
In 1830, there were about
3,000 common schools to
which the poor children were
sent.   In 1833 seventeen
thousand children were being educated by the state
at an expense of forty-two
thousand dollars, and this
attendance increased, so that
in 1860, there were thirty-
one thousand children being

educated at the expense of the state.   Yet there was a
great deal of ignorance, for many persons were unwilling to send their children to school at the expense of
the state, because they would be regarded as paupers.

On his election, Dr. Ruffner at once applied himself
to the organization of the public school system for all
classes of people, and the first law enacted by the legis-

* His election to this responsible position was probably due to the
recommendation of General Robert E. Lee and the support of Major
W. A. Anderson.—See the *Virginia School Journal* for 1902.

lature for the management of the free schools was the work of his hand. Before offering the bill to the legislature he had submitted it for criticism to some of the greatest educators of the North and South, and all agreed that his plan was an excellent one. Dr. Ruffner was also largely responsible for the splendid plan on which the Virginia Polytechnic Institute at Blackburg was organized.

During his administration Dr. Ruffner visited every county in the state except six, lecturing at various places and holding teachers' institutes. After twelve years of service he was removed from office by a change in the politics of the state.

When the State Normal School at Farmville was established for the education of young women to teach in the public schools of Virginia, Dr. Ruffner was elected to the presidency of that institution, and during his three years of service there the training of teachers was so emphasized that the school at Farmville has become a great factor in the educational forces of Virginia.

Since that time Dr. Ruffner has been actively interested in the study of minerals, and in writing a history of Washington and Lee University. He now resides at Lexington, Va. He is a man of vigorous intellect and determined energy, and as Superintendent of Public Instruction he was the right man in the right place. With a less firm and vigorous hand to organize the public school system of Virginia its success could not have been so great. During his term of office the number of children in the public schools increased from 59,000 (1870) to 257,000 (1882), the expenditure for school purposes from $500,-000 to $1,500,000. The impetus thus given to public school education by the hand of Dr. Ruffner has continued, and in 1903 there were in Virginia 375,000 pupils in the public schools at a cost to the state of $2,100,000. There are now 8,965 public schools with 9,044 teachers.*

Illiteracy is fast disappearing from Virginia. About 1840 not more than seventy-five per cent. of the whites over twelve years of age could read and write, but to-day the per cent. has increased to about ninety-two, or over nine-tenths of the total white population. Of course there were a few negroes who could read and write before the war between the states; but by 1900 sixty-seven per cent. of the negro population had received some primary instruction.

* The Public School system is now under the management of a Board of Education, composed of eight members, of whom the Superintendent of Public Instruction is *ex-officio* president. There are now one hundred and seventeen superintendents of schools in the counties and cities, who have a general oversight of the schools. In each county and city there is a school board of citizens who elect the *teachers* and look after the establishment and maintenance of the *schools*.

The interest displayed by Dr. Ruffner, our first Superintendent of Public Instruction, in the education of the masses has been widely felt, and now the leading citizens of our state are advocating universal education. Our state officials, and the leading educators of the schools, colleges and universities, are all eager to lend a helping hand to the primary schools where the boys and girls may be instructed so that they may be better prepared for service. It is to be hoped that in these schools there will always be the spirit of patriotism. May this little book create in the young people of our Commonwealth a desire to imitate our patriots, whose lives so forcibly teach us love for humanity, for our country, and for our God.

Review Questions.

What was the condition of the Virginians at the close of the war ? What did the young Virginians do? Tell of the constitutional convention of 1867. Explain the disfranchising clause and the ironclad oath. When was the public school system established ? Give an account of the life of Dr. Ruffner. Tell of his influence on the schools. How did the attendance in the schools increase ? Tell about the cost of the schools. How are our schools now managed? What spirit should we have in our schools ?

Geography Study.

Map of Virginia.—Find Lexington and Hampden-Sidney. How many counties has Virginia ?

INDEX

Lightning Source UK Ltd.
Milton Keynes UK
UKHW010840030119
334850UK00010B/1345/P